Inspiring and Creative
IDEAS
for Working with Children

INSPIRING AND CREATIVE
IDEAS
FOR WORKING WITH CHILDREN

How to Build Relationships and Enable Change

DEBORAH M. PLUMMER

Jessica Kingsley *Publishers*
London and Philadelphia

First published in 2017
by Jessica Kingsley Publishers
73 Collier Street
London N1 9BE, UK
and
400 Market Street, Suite 400
Philadelphia, PA 19106, USA

www.jkp.com

Library of Congress Cataloging in Publication Data
A CIP catalog record for this book is available from the Library of Congress

British Library Cataloguing in Publication Data
A CIP catalogue record for this book is available from the British Library

ISBN 978 1 84905 651 9
eISBN 978 1 78450 146 4

Printed and bound in Great Britain

Contents

Activities List

Acknowledgements

There are many creative people who have made valuable contributions to this book. Through wide-ranging discussions about training and experiential learning over the years, they have offered the perspectives of parents, teachers, psychologists, social workers, play therapists, speech and language therapists, counsellors, police officers working with vulnerable witnesses and community group leaders.

The use of image-making strategies was originally inspired by Dr Dina Glouberman and by working with my co-practitioners on Imagework training courses.

Many of the ideas that help to make puppets and stories come alive for children have been gleaned from professional story-tellers and puppeteers who have generously shared their knowledge at workshops and courses. There were many students too who valiantly threw themselves into story-telling and puppet-making activities as part of their degree courses in Health Studies and in Evaluating Practice: Working with Children at De Montfort University, Leicester. Their feedback and enthusiasm encouraged me to share my approach through the written word.

My thanks to all these people for sharing their insights.

I also thank all the children and their families who first helped me to formulate my ideas during my work as a speech and language therapist. Their struggles and fortitude have been the true inspiration and motivation for my work.

A Story about Stories

Once upon a time in a faraway place there lived a story-maker who crafted wonderful stories for his family. Every evening, when he had finished his labours and when all the children had eaten their supper and everything had been cleared away, he would sit in his big armchair and listen carefully as each child talked about their day. Then, after pondering on all the events and feelings that he had heard them describe, he would offer them the gift of a story.

In the winter they would sit by the fire in the old kitchen. The story-maker would tell them about countries that the children thought they would never see and about times that were long gone. He told them tales of courage and perseverance, tales about friendships and tales about making wise choices. Sometimes he would take the children on imaginary journeys to different worlds full of magic and wonder. On warm evenings the family would go outside into nature to hear stories about fairies and wood sprites, about the wisdom of plants and animals and about strange mythical creatures. The children loved all these stories and each had a favourite one that had to be told over and over again.

Then one cold, snowy evening, as they prepared to curl up by the fire, the eldest daughter said to her father, 'I am too old for stories now. I have so many tasks to complete every day and I need to spend time with my friends as we have much to talk about before all the spring festivities begin.' The story-maker was sad to hear this. He knew the importance of stories and of stillness and quietness at the end of the busy day. But then he remembered the time that he had said this very same thing to his father many years earlier. The story-maker knew that once a love of stories is planted in children it will develop and flourish in different ways as they grow older. He knew that his daughter would find other times of stillness and quietness in her life. He had every hope that she too would become a story-maker for her own family and community one day. So, the wise story-maker invited his eldest daughter to stay with them by the fire just one more time. And that evening he told a new story...a story about stories.

CHAPTER 1

Context

Inspiring and Creative Ideas for Working with Children draws on both current practice and on activities that have their origins in ancient traditions. Image-making, oral story-telling (in contrast to reading silently or aloud from books) and puppetry all have a rich history.

For centuries they have been employed all over the world as means of promoting family and community values, as aids to self-development and as methods of disseminating community and ancestral knowledge. They are effective tools in facilitative and supportive interactions with children and are still used in many teaching and therapeutic fields today. However, there seems little opportunity for the majority of children to benefit from these wonderful resources on a regular basis.

Recent research[1] and anecdotal evidence suggest that children today are facing greater than ever environmental and personal stresses. These include increasing expectations of their levels of emotional awareness and emotional 'control' at an early age and fewer opportunities for free play with their peers, particularly outdoor play. At the same time, the technological world is continuing to expand and to become more readily accessible. In 'cyberspace' children can, of course, learn skills of reasoning, cooperation and problem-solving. They stretch their imaginations, building amazing worlds and inventing characters with 'back stories' and myriad possibilities for the future. The more problematic side of this is that children could potentially spend much of their leisure time in this way, thus missing out on so many other ways to enjoy and learn about the world and about each other through play.

---

1   See, for example, The Children's Society *The Good Childhood Report 2015*.

It has become only too apparent that misuse of this advanced technology can also result in cyber bullying, lost friendships and crushing 'put downs', which may never have manifested in face-to-face contact or may not have had such devastating and long-lasting effects. We know, for example, that children with recent experiences of being bullied 'have significantly and substantially lower than average subjective well-being' (The Children's Society, 2015, p.26, Table 1).

The world is changing so quickly that most of us who are in a supportive/enabling role with regard to children have experienced a very different way of negotiating childhood to that of today's youngsters. We may feel at a loss as to how to marry the two experiences into a meaningful space for interaction. This is our challenge. The world will continue to change and children will continue to be vulnerable.

I believe that in order to maximise childhood well-being, we need to provide children with quality experiences that will enrich their understanding of the wider world without denying the usefulness and enjoyment that can be gained from engaging with technology. Primarily, this involves us being willing to give our time and energy to creative activities that children *want* to take part in.

Limiting a child's use of computer games, for example, will not be effective in the ways we might want unless there is something else to replace the buzz that he might experience when he achieves the next level, beats his own previous score or wins enough virtual tokens to purchase a magic weapon. In the same way, attempting to reduce a child's excessive use of social media will be an uphill battle unless he has opportunities to experience the enjoyable sense of being in contact with friends through other means.

When a child enjoys getting messy and being creative they need the chance to do this frequently, not just in a half-hour slot on a Tuesday morning! Or, if you believe, as I do, that story-telling and puppetry offer invaluable opportunities for children to learn about themselves, about relationships and about the wider world, then it is important to make the commitment to introducing regular story and puppetry experiences. We need to build these enjoyable experiences into a child's routine so that he looks forward to them and relishes the opportunity to take part as both listener and as a story-teller or puppeteer himself. In an ideal world these opportunities would start at a very early age, but it is never too late.

There are many practical suggestions for activities throughout this book, but no guide of this sort would be complete without also exploring some of the complexities, challenges and joys that we face when we embark on that most special relationship that is involved in supporting children – a relationship that has potential to influence a child's life in ways that we may never know. In order to facilitate effective interactions with children, I believe that we need to:

- know about the challenges that children face and know the strengths and resources that individual children possess

- make every effort to understand the world from the child's point of view and to initiate and respond to communication with children according to this understanding

- know our preferred ways of interacting with children within a safe framework of theory and practice (for example, a teacher might use the activities in this book in a very different way to a parent but nevertheless each will ground the activities in their respective knowledge and experience)

- be clear about what we believe to be the core elements of a helping or nurturing relationship within our personal context

- know our own strengths and be aware of the people, situations and events that we find challenging. This requires skills in self-awareness and the ability to reflect constructively on our thoughts, feelings and actions. Knowing ourselves and understanding our motivations for doing something helps us to be more objective in our understanding of why some things work and others don't

- know the activities. Understanding the value of a chosen activity and the concepts that underpin its use will give us the mechanisms and the confidence to alter it for individual needs.

All these areas are addressed in a variety of ways throughout this book. Over and beyond these, however, there is one more important area for consideration: we also 'know' that alongside the gathering of factual and experiential knowledge, the effectiveness of our interactions with children hinges on something less quantifiable, although still identifiable. The richness of experience that can be derived from creative interactions between adults and children reinforces the view of many that connecting with children in a meaningful way is *an art as well as a science*.

Many discussions with parents, practitioners and students about their engagement with the ideas and their participation in the activities that are presented in this book have consistently highlighted this relationship between knowledge (the 'science' aspect) and intuitive action that is based on that knowledge (the 'art' aspect).

Each person's experiences underline how this relationship is relevant for all our interactions with children whether they be in family, teaching, therapeutic or community settings.

The art of an interaction is what happens in the 'in-between' when we enter into a relationship in which one person has a primarily supportive role in relation to the other. In the 'in-between', our knowledge and experience melds with our attitudes and intentions; we meet the other person – child or adult – with all *his* knowledge, experience, attitudes and intentions and find a way of interacting that is caring, safe and respectful. We come together in a shared activity that bridges the diverse worlds of adults and children.

This is where imagination, creativity and insight flourish for both participants; this is where image-making, story-telling and puppetry can play a unique and rewarding role.

Using this book

The information and activities in this book have been organised in a way that encourages you to build your experience in a gradual manner, giving you plenty of time to try out the different ideas and to reflect on their relevance for your own situation.

As you will see, the basic philosophy of the activities is evident in other supportive and enabling strategies too. This is an important point. The creative use of the imagination should not be seen as something completely different to, or separate from, the down-to-earth principles that apply to all our interactions with children.

Each of the main *exploratory activities* that you are asked to complete is followed by examples of how to adapt this activity for use with children. The adaptations are marked as either *general* adaptations or *story-telling and puppetry* adaptations. Throughout the book you will also find *image-making activities and guidelines*, which will help you to ensure that the activities feel safe for children, *story-building activities* (relevant for both oral stories and puppet plays) and *story* and *puppetry pointers*, which offer practical tips on setting up story times and on handling puppets.

There is a selection of 'neuro nuggets' featured throughout the book. These offer bite-sized examples of the information available to us from the work of neuroscientists.

I have also included samples of conversations with children. These samples highlight ways in which we can be mindful of the language of possibility and change. However, none of the activities are intended to be used as ways for 'getting children to talk' if they don't want to.

I suggest that you keep a notebook for your thoughts and drawings so that you can refer back to them. Move on when it feels right to do so. Gradually, your notebook jottings will come together so that by the time you have completed the book, you will feel confident in using image-making and puppetry[2] in a variety of ways and you will have crafted one or more oral stories. These will give you the basis for many more.

The crafting of stories and plays as supportive means to help children to grow and change initially takes time and care. *However*, and I cannot

---

2   In this book I am not covering aspects of using puppets and dolls in relation to child protection issues. This requires specific training, although undoubtedly some of the basic principles outlined will still apply.

emphasise this point enough, **using imagery, telling stories and playing with puppets are all beautiful, natural ways to engage with children**.

If you are not already using these tools please don't wait until you have completed the book before plunging in and using them as a fun way to celebrate the gift of imagination with a child. The ability to imagine is one of the most precious personal resources that any of us possesses. A vivid imagination, a love of stories and temporary immersion in a world of make-believe are all part of a healthy childhood and adult experience. Using imagery, playing with puppets and telling stories with no goals in mind other than enjoyment will add to this experience for both you and the children. It will also help you to feel relaxed and confident about utilising these tools for specific purposes at other times.

References

Aveyard, H. and Sharp, P. (2009) *A Beginner's Guide to Evidence Based Practice in Health and Social Care*. Maidenhead: Open University Press, McGraw Hill Education.

The Children's Society (2015) *The Good Childhood Report 2015*. London: The Children's Society.

CHAPTER 2

Meeting the Protagonists

At this point I want to introduce four children who will feature throughout the book. Ardan[3], Aisha, Morag and Ben reflect some of the many aspects of troubled and stressed children that each of us might encounter in our work or in our community. These four children, differing in age and background, do not represent any particular child or family that I have ever met or know of. Their fictional experiences are, however, based on observations that I have gathered during many years of working with children of all ages in various settings.

We start with the perspective of key adults in the life of each of these four children. As you read through the brief outlines you might find yourself thinking about how you would begin to build a supportive relationship with each child, the feelings that you might have and the possible challenges you and the children might be facing. You might make a few notes so that you can refer back to them and add to them as you find out more in subsequent chapters. Your experiences of engaging with these children will help you to expand and adapt the ideas presented throughout the book. You will find that this is the case even if your prime interest lies with only one age group.

Ben (aged 4)

Introduced by Mel and Greg, Ben's parents.

> *He is our little miracle! We had almost given up on the idea of ever having our own child, so Ben has been all the more special. He was six weeks early, such a tiny scrap, and he had such struggles*

---

3   Some aspects of Ardan's case study originally appeared in Plummer (2014). Morag's experience of playing musical chairs was used as an example in Plummer (2015).

in his first few months. He still has difficulties with coordinating his movements. Now he is seeing an educational psychologist. She thinks that he is behind in his learning for his age. He won't play near other children and cries constantly when he's with any other adult except us. But, surely that's to be expected with all that he's been through?

Morag (aged 7)

Introduced by Jo, special needs support staff.

I was the observer/note-taker that day. We had been particularly concerned about Morag as she seemed to be slipping back in her learning. She was taking part in a game of musical chairs – a fun game that Sarah and I had chosen to help the children with their listening skills. The children had just finished a reading and understanding task. Morag had done well with this but is generally very self-critical with regard to her abilities. For example, she frequently refers to herself as being 'rubbish' at reading. In fact, now that I think about it, she often says 'I can't do that' or 'I'm rubbish' these days. Nevertheless, during the game she managed to get to a chair every time the music stopped and she seemed to be enjoying herself until there were only three children playing and two chairs left to sit on. Then she suddenly burst into tears. I rushed forward to see what happened. 'I hurt my elbow,' she said through her sobs. No one saw this happen but we ended the game and checked her arm – nothing broken thank goodness – not even a bruise. She sat with me for the rest of the session and went back to her classroom when we had finished as if nothing had happened.

Aisha (aged 10)

Introduced by Laura, Aisha's mother.

My child, Aisha, is very shy and quiet. We have tried to encourage her to mix with more children from her class, arranging play sessions after school with some of the other kids and parents, enrolling her in a dance class and so on, but she finds these activities really difficult and tends to just watch the others and not join in. I don't want to put too much pressure on her. She loves being at home with us and spends hours on the computer playing games. We have made sure that these are age appropriate of course. I think they are helping her with her learning, but I am concerned that she is spending so long sitting in front of a screen. It is very difficult to restrict her usage of the computer. It is one of the few things that she seems to enjoy.

Ardan (aged 14)

Introduced by Tom, Ardan's speech and language therapist.

Ardan was 14 when he first came to see me. He arrived at the speech therapy clinic with his mother. It was 4.30 and he had come straight from school, he was still wearing his school uniform – evidently a very new blazer but muddy trousers and well-worn shoes. He looked older than 14, tall for his age.

Ardan's family, originally from Ireland, had moved five times during his early life, the last move being just six months prior to his appointment with me. The notes that accompanied him indicated that he was first seen by a speech and language therapist when he was three years old. He had been referred by his GP over concerns that he had suddenly developed a marked stammer. The severity of his stammer had fluctuated a great deal during the intervening years. The therapist who saw him briefly just before his last move, had noted that currently his stammering consisted of frequent, rapid repetitions of syllables (Mon-Mon-Mon-Mon-Monday) and long silent 'blocks' during which his face would contort with tension as he tried to force out a troublesome word.

During our first meeting it became clear that Ardan had tried several different methods to help him to feel more in control of his speech and to build his confidence. It was also evident that his attempts at coping with his stammering and the unstinting support of his parents had given him some temporary relief. But with each move, each new school, each new friendship group, the stress of communication was increasing. He was failing at school and was becoming more and more withdrawn. His feelings of failure and anxiety were exacerbating his speech difficulty; his self-esteem was at an all time low.

Ardan, Morag, Aisha and Ben each have unique stories to tell, but they also have much in common. Each child is struggling to make sense of his or her world and each is at a critical stage of development emotionally, mentally and physically. Similarly, Tom, Mel, Greg, Jo and Laura will bring different experiences, knowledge, attitudes and intentions to his or her relationships with the children. What can Aisha's mother do to help her daughter to build emotional resilience and make wise choices when faced with today's stresses? What can parents and practitioners do to help children like Ben to engage in supportive relationships and to enable change in therapeutic and teaching environments? What about appropriate support for Morag who, it transpires, is trying to cope with enormous stresses at home in the best ways that she can? And then there is Ardan, who has difficulties trusting adults enough to be able to tell his story or to feel that he can rely on another person to help him when things are tough.

Although the adults have very different roles within each child's world, what they all have in common is a desire to understand the children and to support them in the best possible way. Providing the optimum supportive environment in which a child can feel nurtured and respected takes skill and dedication. Much of what we do as a skilled helper is common sense but there is also a great deal that can be learned and developed.

References

Plummer, D. (2014) 'Supporting healthy self-esteem.' *BACP Children and Young People* (June).
Plummer, D. (2015) 'Mindful Games.' In C. Willard and A. Saltzman (eds) *Teaching Mindfulness Skills to Kids and Teens*. New York: The Guilford Press.

CHAPTER 3

Twelve Principles for Building Relationships and Enabling Change

1. Enabling relationships are child-centred

As a major part of our role as parent, teacher, therapist, mentor or carer, we are aiming for an 'enabling' relationship. In this respect our aims will be similar to those of a counsellor and his client, aims that lead to the child feeling empowered, growing in his understanding of himself, living in a more effective and resourceful way and having a greater sense of well-being. All these benefits should be long-lasting (Sanders, 2002).

The principles outlined by Carl Rogers (1961) are widely accepted as being an important aspect of an enabling relationship. These underpin my own approach and are therefore evident throughout the activities in this book. Rogers, the originator of 'person-centred' therapy, believed that each of us has a natural tendency to strive to achieve our full potential in life and he proposed that there are certain conditions that will promote this tendency.

These became known as the 'core conditions' for a successful therapeutic alliance, but Rogers also made it clear that he felt such conditions were valid for *all* human relationships. He believed that if he maintained a relationship characterised on his part by congruence ('a genuineness and transparency, in which I am my real feelings'), unconditional positive regard ('warm acceptance of and prizing of the other person as a separate individual') and empathy ('a sensitive ability to see his world and himself

19

as he sees them') then the other person in the relationship would be more self-directing and self-confident and able to cope with life's problems 'more comfortably' (Rogers, 1961, pp.37–8).

With these core conditions in mind, one way to consider the use of image-making, story-telling and puppetry with children is with a sense of shared enjoyment. We could think of them as gifts to the child, gifts that will enhance his world and help him to flourish. What makes a gift special? You will have thought about it carefully, getting a feel for what the child would really like, rather than what you would like if you were his age (empathy). You would perhaps wrap your gift in special paper, add ribbons or divide it up into several smaller packages so as to prolong the enjoyment and show that you value the child (prizing of the other person).

The ways in which you do this will draw on your creativity and your knowledge of the child. Perhaps you would savour the pleasure of the gift alongside the child, watching his expressions, sharing his excitement. This will involve a letting go of any personal, emotional investment in the gift, such as: 'I have put so much effort into this I will be upset if he doesn't engage with it.' A special gift can be simple or elaborate. Just liked a well-loved comfort toy, it might be something that a child will return to again and again. Or it could be something that serves its purpose and is then put aside. Perhaps your gift would be something that both you and the child can add to over time; maybe it is something that he can experiment with or use in different ways. If we approach image-making, story-telling and puppetry in this child-centred way, with respect and with the right intentions, I believe that we cannot go far wrong.

2. Enabling relationships are based on trust and respect

A safe environment in which children can grow and learn is based on respect for each child's uniqueness and a genuine wish to try to understand his thoughts, feelings and behaviours. It also requires a great deal of trust on their part: trust that we won't let them down, that we will take their concerns seriously and that we won't judge them or criticise them. Building trust is of major importance. How might we do this? Primarily we help children to build healthy trust through our *actions*. Evidence is important for children. We may feel respect, we may value each individual, but if we do not convey this to them or if the respect and value is not *felt/perceived* by them, then the impact will be lessened. We need to *show* them that we are interested in them as unique individuals, that we truly care about their welfare and that we will respect their thoughts and feelings.

Even seemingly unrelated aspects within the environment can have an effect on a child's perception of respect and trust. For example, the way that we take care of ourselves and any equipment we might use (such as puppets and toys) also reflects what we feel about the children and that we value them enough to make things special for them.

Early years support worker, Caroline, had been observing Ben's language and his construction skills during play:

> It took Ben a long time to set up the farm in just the way that he wanted, building complex-shaped fields edged by plastic fences. He asked me very earnestly to keep it this way so that it would be the same when he played with it the next day. While coping with the frustration of someone else playing with your toys is an important part of developing emotional resilience, this was not something that I needed to introduce on top of the frustration that he was already dealing with. Knowing that the farm would be played with by other children that afternoon, I took a photograph of the layout and set up the farm in the same way just before his arrival. I wasn't sure if he would really remember, but I hoped that I was showing that I appreciated his inventive work and that I took his request seriously.

3. A child's developmental level and personal circumstances are more relevant than chronological age

A child's developmental level may be very different to that expected of the average child of his age. This is particularly true of many children who have suffered neglect in their early years. Children with learning difficulties and children with specific speech and language difficulties are vulnerable too. They may not yet have the language to be able to reason, problem-solve, negotiate and so on.

Some children are ahead of the 'average' expected for their age or may have mixed abilities – advanced in some areas and struggling in others. There are also children who are not reaching their full potential because of current stressful circumstances. The infinite variations in ability, developmental stage and life circumstances mean that there will always be times when you will need to adapt activities for different children (see pages 115–116).

4. Developing our skills of observation and listening will help us to tune into a child's needs

Morag: I have to help Mummy. Sometimes I get it wrong and she gets very sad. I think about her lots, even when I'm at school. There are lots of things I can't do. I wish I was cleverer so I could help Mummy more.

 Neuro nugget

When stress is excessive or continuous over a long period of time, even at relatively low levels, then we will experience a 'toxic' build up of stress hormones such as cortisol, which is released by the adrenal glands. Cortisol plays a part in raising blood glucose levels and in breaking down fat and other proteins to provide extra energy for the fight/flight reaction. However, high levels of cortisol can affect our memory capacity and will dampen our immune system. This coupled with a fall in levels of dopamine and serotonin (feel-good hormones) in the pre-frontal cortex can cause us to feel 'overwhelmed, fearful, and miserable, colouring our thoughts, feelings, and perceptions with a sense of threat or dread, as if everything we need to do is far too hard' (Sunderland, 2006, p.87).

Because every child develops at a different rate and under different circumstances, the only way to respond appropriately to a child's attempts to make sense of his world is to observe and listen mindfully 'in the moment' and to be guided by what happens as a result.

Charles Tart refers to this type of mindfulness as a form of 'perceptual intelligence'. Tart makes a clear distinction between consideration of others shown through conditioning or 'habit' and the more awakened ability to 'see more accurately and discriminatingly and so behave more appropriately toward others and toward our inner selves' (Tart, 1994, p.6). I find this a useful phrase to help me to think about how we each perceive and make sense of all the elements of an interaction and how we use this information to engage in meaningful, healthy relationships.

Perceptual intelligence involves both awareness of the other person and self-awareness. For example, I say something to a child that causes their face to 'light up'. I note my own response to this reaction. I take note of what it was that I said, I think about why this particular interchange appeared to work well for this child and I wonder how I can capitalise on this.

I see two children engaged in make-believe play. They are totally absorbed in a natural give and take of conversation between two puppet animals. Should I join with them? What is my motivation for doing that?

I might set out to tell a story with a group of children. I am feeling tired and I am worried that one of the group is uncharacteristically boisterous and may 'spoil' the story for the others. If I am being self-aware, not only will I tune into the child's behaviour as an indication of his thoughts and emotions, I will also tune into my own thoughts and feelings. Why do I consider his behaviour disruptive? How will I handle this? Would I do it differently if I was feeling more on top of things? (See also Story pointer 6.1.)

> *Aisha's mother recognised that she frequently referred to Aisha as a 'shy' child. Reflecting on more specific behaviours helped her to think about possible ways to help: 'At the moment she is unsure of herself when she first arrives somewhere new. It takes her a long while to build the confidence to talk to new people.' Being more specific about behaviour and feelings can open up avenues for appropriate support: 'It might help if we practised some things that she could say.'*

It would be impossible to be perceptually alert in every situation and every interaction but it also doesn't need to be hard work. Once you are aware of what to look out for, the actual 'noticing' can become almost automatic, and we always have an opportunity to reflect on an interaction after the event if we have not been able to do so at the time.

5. Active listening is a skill that takes practice

> *Ardan: No one really understands what it's like to stammer. I have so much that I want to say, so much that I want to tell people. Sometimes I want to shout 'I'm not stupid! Just shut up and listen!' Once at one of my schools there was this other kid who stammered too. He was the only one who knew how hard it can be.*

Sometimes our own thoughts, feelings and preconceptions can get in the way of listening accurately to someone else. Active listening requires us to filter out such distractions, put our own concerns to one side and really focus on the speaker. Not only do we hear the words that the speaker is using, we also look for non-verbal signals. We note his body posture, level of eye contact and gestures. We listen to his intonation and emphasis. All these aspects allow us the opportunity to get a better understanding of what the speaker means.

Active listening also involves *showing* that we are listening and genuinely interested in what someone has to say. This will also be evident through non-verbal signals such as eye contact, gestures and body posture, coupled with thoughtful comments and sensitive (but infrequent) questions that will encourage him to elaborate on what he is saying.

Some common blocks to active listening in a counselling situation are also relevant to working with children, in particular, being too quick to reassure ('Don't worry, it will all be okay'), denying feelings ('Don't be silly, there's nothing to be worried about'), jumping in with advice ('Well, if I were you I would…'), arguing logically ('There is no point in being anxious because…') and asking too many questions ('Why did you do that?' 'Why do you feel angry?'). Engaging with image-making, puppetry and story-telling is an effective way of avoiding all these pitfalls.

I always felt in a very privileged position to be able to give children my individual attention during therapy sessions and in small groups. I appreciate how much harder this is in a classroom or other large group situations. The good news is that even brief moments of 'being heard', acknowledged, understood and accepted can add coinage to a child's sense of self and to his emotional well-being and open the way for building a supportive relationship.

6. We need to be aware of children's abilities to understand and use verbal communication

Being child-centred in our intentions will usually lead to us communicating appropriately with children. However, there may be times when, despite our best efforts, there seems to be a loss of understanding or a discordant communication.

As with most things in life, it takes a while for children to fine tune their understanding of all the different subtleties of adult speech. Each child reaches that understanding, and perfects his ability to respond appropriately, at different times. As an example, if you are playing with a two-year-old and he has in front of him a doll and a cup and you say 'Let's give dolly a drink' (perhaps even inadvertently looking directly from the cup to the doll), when the child picks up the cup and gives the doll a drink it might be because of all the non-verbal cues inherent in the play situation. It could be that you could give the same instruction in a language unknown to the child and he will still respond appropriately.

Here's another example. 'Before you put on your shoes, run upstairs and and brush your teeth will you?' Before and after concepts may not develop until around six years of age although they can be very well understood by some children at a much younger age. A child with a specific language disorder may not fully understand this concept until even later.

Try saying 'maybe' in response to a child requesting a trip to the park. 'Maybe' (meaning, if you're good for the rest of the day) sounds different to 'Maybe' (that sounds like a good idea, we'll see how it goes) or 'Maybe' (I can't think about that right now)! The changes in intonation, eye contact and posture might be quite subtle. Not all children are able to pick this up.

Some children feel awkward asking for help if they have not understood. They prefer to watch and follow the lead of other children. They may *pretend* that they have understood you or have understood the task or the game that you have introduced. It is best to take responsibility for this by encouraging children to tell you if you have not explained something clearly. This helps to avoid the problem of children feeling that *they* have failed.

It can sometimes be helpful to tune into the *type* of words that a child is using too. This takes a little bit of practice but the basic guideline is to ask yourself if the language that a child is using at any one time is mostly:

- visual: I *saw* the long queue, I *see* what you mean

- auditory: I *heard* the crowds; I'm *buzzing*

- feeling: I *felt sick* with excitement, I *feel it* in my bones
- action centred: I *walked* up to the ride, I *blocked* out the memory.

Note the difference between Morag and Aisha, both of whom are retelling an enjoyable experience on a fairground ride:

Morag: The wait felt like forever, I was all shivery and excited.

Aisha: I had to wait a long time. I thought it might be good fun.
My hands were shaking.

Let's say I was helping the two girls to explore various emotions through the medium of puppets. My puppet's response to Morag's description would reinforce the feeling element and might be something like: 'I get the feeling it was a great ride but felt a bit scary too!' (She may, of course, reject the scary bit, but I am suggesting a possible range of feelings for a single event.) However, if I go straight for feelings in response to Aisha's description she might think that I don't really 'get it' so I might start out with: 'I think my hands would shake too.' I would then introduce some possible reasons for my hands shaking: '…because I would be a bit scared and excited at the same time! I wonder if that's what you were thinking.' In this example I use 'think' and pick up on her observations to try and match her own language.

7. Thoughts, emotions and behaviour are closely linked

Age and experience will naturally affect the depth and range of feeling words available to children. A child may be feeling frustrated or anxious, for example, but not know how to express this appropriately. Imagine if Ben had the ability to describe his experiences of his world. What might be the key elements? Perhaps 'confusing', 'unpredictable', 'overwhelming', 'frustrating' or 'anxiety-provoking'. The less verbal skills a child has and the more overwhelming the emotion, the more likely he is to show his feelings through his (often challenging) behaviour. Such displays of anxiety, anger or upset by one child may trigger feelings of anxiety, anger or distress in another. It will be the adult's task to help children to regulate their emotions and demonstrate a calm way of reacting to any displays of strong emotion.

8. A child's motivation to communicate with us may be hampered by current circumstances or previous experiences

Children are motivated to engage in a communication for many different reasons – because they want to: convey information about the environment and about what they hear and see ('Look Mummy, a train', 'I've just learnt about the stars'), convey emotions and physical feelings ('I hate soup!', 'I feel sick'), ask a question ('How does this work?'), make a request ('Can I go to the park?'), explain ('It wasn't my fault. It just fell over!'), comment ('I'm building a big bridge', 'Jack is older than me'), refuse ('No! Don't want to!'), answer a question ('I think it's in my school bag') or negotiate ('If you do this bit then I'll finish this bit'). If a child has had experience of being consistently ignored, ridiculed or punished for initiating any of these interactions they will learn to stay quiet and their motivation to interact with a new person will be severely hampered. Patience and the provision of ample opportunities for communication can turn this situation around.

9. Silence is golden

Times of silence, pausing during your own speech and making comments more often than you ask questions will give children valuable opportunities to both initiate an interaction and respond effectively.

How often have you heard yourself or someone else ask a child several questions in a row? 'What did you do at school today? Did you have fun? Was your friend there? The one you always play with...what's his name?' Or 'What time do you have to be there? Did you write it down? How am I supposed to know if you don't tell me these things?' This is a lot to process and can put a child under pressure quite simply because they are not yet able to hold so much information in memory or because they are already full of emotion and are not able to take in so many questions and think how to respond at the same time.

If you do ask a question, consider asking an open question that could lead to a more elaborated response, rather than a closed question requiring unelaborated responses such as 'yes/no' or that leads to answers that can be judged as either 'correct' or 'incorrect'. For instance, note the difference in the following versions of an interaction between Ardan and Tom:

> *Ardan: He started it.*
>
> *Tom: Was he making fun of you because of your stammer?*
>
> *Ardan: Yeah.*
>
> *Tom: So you got detention. And that's happened before hasn't it?*
>
> *Ardan: Yeah.*

Or:

> *Ardan: He started it*
>
> *Tom: So, this other boy wanted to pick a fight. I wonder if you feel okay to tell me what happened (inviting a story).*
>
> *Ardan: Him and his mates were calling me 'stutter head'. It's always happening. They think it's funny.*
>
> *Tom: They were making fun of you and you got angry.*
>
> *(pause)*
>
> *Ardan: School sucks! I can't even answer the register.*
>
> *Tom: It sounds like there are a ton of things that get you fired up about this new school (pause). We can work on stuff together so that you feel more okay about it if you like.*
>
> *(Ardan looks down at his hands.)*
>
> *Tom: We'll take it one step at a time!*

10. The ways in which we show appreciation of a child's efforts need careful consideration

EXPLORATORY ACTIVITY 3.1: PRAISE AND APPRECIATION

- What images does the word 'praise' conjure up for you?
- How do you feel when you are praised?
- Is there anything that you particularly enjoy being praised for?
- Is there anything that you do not like to be praised for?
- Are you more comfortable accepting praise from some people than from others? If so, why do you think this is?
- How do you praise/reward yourself? Is this effective?
- Do you have any positive memories of your peers showing you their appreciation when you were a child? In what ways did they show their appreciation? What effect did this have?
- How do you praise children? What effects have you noticed?
- How do you show your appreciation of a child's contributions to your day?

Appropriate appreciation and reward strategies have always been a central aspect of my work and I am still adding to and refining my thoughts about this. The pros and cons of praising children seems to be a topic that crops up in the media at regular intervals with questions such as 'Do we have a tendency to over-praise children?' and 'Should we mix praise and constructive feedback at a certain ratio?' Genuine appreciation and constructive feedback help children to learn and grow in confidence and motivation, but, once again, given the diversity of children's personalities, strengths and needs there cannot be an exact formula for this. The *way* in which we give feedback needs some careful consideration however, since we want to help children to internalise our acceptance and thus promote *self*-acceptance.

EXPLORATORY ACTIVITY 3.2: ALTERNATIVES TO PRAISE

Think of five words or phrases that you might use as an alternative to 'praise'. How do they differ in quality? For example, does appreciation have a different feel to it compared with praise? Is there a different feel to 'You completed that task in good time' and 'I appreciate your efforts in finishing the task in good time'?

Being specific

One well-used guideline for giving feedback is to make it genuine, simple, specific and descriptive: 'I liked the way you listened to what Morag had to say about the story. You looked at her while she was talking and you asked a great question afterwards', 'Thank you for being so supportive to Ben when he got upset. That worked well because he calmed down straight away' or 'Your "problem" picture shows me what it must feel like to be worried about everything. This is what I call thoughtful.'

Being specific also includes encouraging children to give specific, descriptive feedback to others: 'What did you like about the way that Morag told us that?' For many children, peer recognition can prove to be more meaningful and more motivating than feedback from adults.

Similarly, it is helpful to encourage descriptive *self*-evaluation: 'I talked to someone new at break time and it was hard but I felt good afterwards.' This is not the same as boasting. It is a way of children recognising the changes that they are making and reducing their reliance on praise from others.

Expressing your admiration or appreciation of a child's spontaneous activities can enable a child to make positive self-evaluations about things that they might otherwise take for granted: 'I noticed you on your skateboard just now. That takes really good balance. How did you know how to do that?', 'I had no idea that you could make a kite. Was that hard to learn?', 'Tim said that you always remember people's birthdays – that's really great – such a friendly thing to do.' I have been known to be a little over-effusive in my comments at times – beware of this as it can sound contrived and children will be quick to pick up on it!

All the aspects of a nurturing relationship explored in Chapter 9 are also relevant in this context.

11. Children want to be able to predict responses

We generally seek to make our worlds as predictable and controllable as possible so that we will know how to act and react. We look for information about specific relationships between events and consequences – about cause and effect – and this starts from a very early age. 'When I throw my sock out of the buggy you pick it up' or 'When I cry, you cuddle me.' Over time, we begin to attribute certain characteristics to people around us, particularly where their behaviour and the intention behind that behaviour appear to be consistent: 'You shouted at me because you think I am bad.' For many vulnerable children the attribution is more likely to be self-directed: 'You shouted at me because I *am* bad.' By making these links a child can predict how others might respond to similar situations in the future: 'If you are angry I know that you will shout at me.' Children want to be able to *anticipate* the effects that their behaviour and other people's behaviour will have. This means that a child may feel at a loss if a key adult in his life is very unpredictable, perhaps being tolerant of certain behaviours on some days, but angry or impatient about the same behaviours at other times.

Experimenting with and experiencing new ways of thinking and new ways of doing things is part of the natural process of growing up, but it can be a particularly scary prospect for young and vulnerable children. Changes and unpredictability constantly upend the schema that they are trying to construct about how the world works. Each time a child comes across a new experience, a new way of an adult behaving with him, he is likely to have an immediate gut reaction as to whether or not it fits with his 'framework' of understanding. This natural selection process will influence his motivation to engage with someone new and can severely hamper our initial attempts at constructing a supportive relationship.

Once again, the key is to create an atmosphere where children can feel safe and respected and where we aim to be as consistent in our attitudes and intentions as possible.

12. We can only do our best

Be kind to yourself if things don't go as you expect and celebrate when they do!

References

Rogers, C. (1961) *On Becoming a Person: A Therapist's View of Psychotherapy*. London: Constable.

Sanders, P. (2002) *First Steps in Counselling: A Students' Companion for Basic Introductory Courses* (3rd edition). Ross-on-Wye: PCCS Books.

Sunderland, M. (2006) *The Science of Parenting*. London: Dorling Kindersley.

Tart, C. T. (1994) *Living the Mindful Life: A Handbook for Living in the Present Moment*. Boston, MA: Shambhala Publications Inc.

CHAPTER 4

Imagination and Creativity

Laura: We went to Aisha's school yesterday for parent's evening. They are very pleased with her academic progress, especially her reading and writing. They said what we already knew – she comes up with amazingly imaginative stories for her age.

Their biggest concern seems to be her difficulties in mixing with the other children. She is a real 'loner' and doesn't cope with group activities at all well. She's a bit like me in that respect.

Our task as supporters and enablers is to help children to negotiate their way through the world and to create for themselves a life story that promotes psychological well-being. As they experiment with cause and effect, learn about other people, learn about their environment and begin to formulate their beliefs, we are there to give a helping hand. When a child makes an erroneous connection between events, we can help her to revision the situation. If a child has had a difficult start in life that is leading to her experiencing overwhelmingly negative thoughts, then we are there to help her to rewrite her personal script.

What happens when children and adults interact in this way will depend to a large extent on our ability to employ the art of imagination. Every one of us has the ability to imagine and every one of us has the capacity to use imagination in a constructive way as an important component of supportive relationships. Imagination allows us to be more effective in directing our attention both internally (to images, feelings and thoughts) and externally (to our environment and to other people).

By cultivating a 'therapeutic imagination' we can strengthen our understanding of what it might be like to *be* the child with whom we are working and start to understand how they might experience the world. We can then monitor and shape our interactions accordingly. Psychologist and Jungian analyst, James Hillman, has written extensively in the field of imaginal psychology. In *Healing Fiction* he talks of the therapy process that occurs between therapist and client as being most successful when there is 'a collaboration between fictions, a revisioning of the story into a…more imaginative plot' (Hillman, 1983, pp.17–8). Hillman is referring to the idea that we construct our own meanings in life. There are no 'bare events, plain facts, simple data' as he puts it (p.23); it is how we perceive and interpret these events, facts and data that matters. Viewing our interactions as helping children to 'revision' their story makes sense, and the activities of image-making, story-telling and puppetry are eminently suited to this task.

I also view promoting the development of imagination in children to be a necessity, not a luxury. By encouraging children to see the value of imagination, we can help them to develop *their* understanding of people, situations and events and to develop their abilities to understand their own thoughts and actions: 'The way we imagine our lives is the way we are going to live our lives. For the manner in which we tell ourselves about what is going on is the genre through which events become experiences' (Hillman, 1983, p.23).

EXPLORATORY ACTIVITY 4.1: IMAGINATION

(This could also be carried out as a discussion or as a drawing activity.)

On a large sheet of paper write the word 'imagination'. Around or underneath this write anything that comes to mind with regard to this concept. What does imagination mean to you? If possible, discuss your thoughts with someone else. Do you each have similar views about imagination or are there variations that indicate a different type of relationship with this concept?

GENERAL ADAPTATION

Based on your thoughts while completing Exploratory activity 4.1, think how you might talk about imagination with children. You might start by asking them to think of times when they have imagined something that they couldn't actually see or hear. What about a story, a poem or a drawing of a 'made-up' animal? You might talk about how we can experience a feeling like sadness or anger or being happy just by imagining something and how we can use our imaginations in a helpful way, for example by visualising ourselves doing something that is difficult and feeling okay about it.

Jo chose to introduce the idea of 'visualising' with the whole group, rather than with Morag alone. She felt that it would be useful for the other children and she wanted to help Morag understand that her feelings were quite natural:

> *There are lots of things that happen to us and around us that help us to feel okay about ourselves, but sometimes we can feel unhappy about ourselves too. We might start to think 'I can't do this' or 'I'm no good at this' or 'everyone has more friends than me'. If this happens then your imagination can help you to feel better about yourself again and it can help you to actually get to be better at doing some of the hard things.*

She then used the following activity, which is based on a well-known exercise demonstrating the potential of visualisation in relation to a physical achievement.

> *Imagine that you are a cat. When cats have been sitting still for a while or when they have been asleep they like to stretch out from their noses to their tails. See if you can stretch like a cat. Kneel down with your hands on the floor in front of you. Gradually begin to*

stretch your arms forward, walking your hands along the floor, feel your body getting longer and longer. Now bring your hands back to just in front of you and start to stretch out your legs behind you instead. First one and then the other. Now lie on your back on the floor and stretch out your arms, spread your fingers as wide as they'll go. Stretch out your legs and point your toes towards the other side of the room. Now let everything relax again. Gently roll over onto your side and then very slowly sit up. Now curl yourself up into a ball and when I say 'go' uncurl and stand up, reach up towards the ceiling as high as you can, really stretching your fingers upwards and standing on tiptoes. 'Go.' Well done! Now relax again and slowly curl up in a ball. I want to show you how clever your mind is. Instead of really stretching this time I want you to imagine that you are uncurling and reaching for the ceiling. You can reach right up way above your head. You can touch the ceiling. You're so good at stretching you can go much further than you thought was possible. In your imagination feel what it's like to stretch that far. See yourself doing it… Good. Now I want you to really uncurl and stretch up and see how far you go. When you imagined doing this you told your body that it could stretch much further than the first time you did it…and it worked!

Now relax and then give yourself a little shake all over. Shake your arms and your hands. Shake your legs and your feet, shake your shoulders, shake your body and rest quietly on the floor for a moment.

(From Plummer, 2010, p.53)

The link with creativity

Imagination is closely linked to creativity. This connection is mediated by our personal belief systems concerning the nature of creativity in relation to our view of ourselves. Creativity is therefore a subjective concept – it will mean different things to different people.

Some time ago I helped out at a regular family craft session run in the local community hall. I offered puppet-making as one of the table-top activities. During the first session we used wooden spoons, paints and a basket full of scraps of material and wool. Parents and grandparents took part to varying degrees. Some made the puppets for their children, following the child's instructions as to where to paint the eyes, what colour wool to use for the hair and so on. Others sat next to their child and gently encouraged or helped when asked. Some parents made their own puppet alongside their child. For some parents and grandparents, it was a liberating experience; others found it daunting. A few remarked that they hadn't done any sticking and painting since their own childhood. One parent said that she didn't want to make a puppet because she was not creative enough. This was not what I had hoped for a family craft session.

So, while we still needed an overall structure or theme (complete freedom to do whatever you want can also feel overwhelming and inhibiting for some people), subsequent sessions became much more free-flowing and creative. We would pile up a selection of various materials and see what children came up with in association with a general theme such as animals and birds, or heroes and heroines. One child wanted to make a flapping bird and another child's father showed us how to fold the paper wings. Someone's big sister showed us how to add a weight to a paper snake to make it move like a puppet. The table became a buzz of conversation between parents and children and there was no thought of getting things 'right'. We were just using our imaginations freely, experimenting and playing to strengths. The result was that children often went home with much more inventive, creative puppets than during the first session. On the other hand, there were one or two children who made wooden spoon puppets every session until they had a small family of them, each with its own unique character. It was just as important that they were able to choose to do this.

The connections that we make between imagination and creativity often depend on feelings of confidence. For instance, although I might consider myself to be imaginative, my aim of becoming more creative in my interactions with a child could be influenced by how confident I feel in my own creative abilities, my confidence in the intrinsic efficacy of the activities I have chosen and my level of confidence in my knowledge of the child. My experiences of the family craft session encouraged me to revision these elements and to remember that where imagination and creativity are able to flourish, there really is no right or wrong way of doing things.

EXPLORATORY ACTIVITY 4.2: CREATIVITY

How would you complete the following sentences? Aim for three different ideas for each one.

- When I am feeling creative I can…
- When I encourage creativity in children I feel…
- When I see (specify child's name) being creative I know that…

Laura completed this activity after a discussion with the mother of another child in Aisha's class. Both women were keen to encourage creative activities at home with their girls. Laura's responses triggered a further conversation about ways in which her view of her own creative energy could be an important contributory factor in nurturing Aisha's imagination:

> *When I am feeling creative I can come up with great stories, solve problems, interact with Aisha entertainingly; when I encourage creativity in children I feel satisfied: a job done well, energised, optimistic about their future; when I see Aisha being creative I know that she is happy, confident and learning.*

STORY-TELLING AND PUPPETRY ADAPTATION

This idea can be adapted for an individual or group activity with children. For example, at the end of a story-telling or puppetry session children could take turns to complete a series of sentences such as:

- Today I was creative when...
- Being creative helped me to...
- While I was doing a drawing about the story I learnt that...

EXPLORATORY ACTIVITY 4.3: CREATIVITY PYRAMID

This activity is based on an exercise from Personal Construct Theory (Kelly, 1955; Dalton and Dunnett, 2005). It is one of many ways to look in more detail at how we construe aspects of our world.

Think of a person whom you consider to be creative. At the top of a large sheet of paper write down four attributes that this person possesses that cause you to view him/her as creative. You could start off by thinking 'she demonstrates her creativity by...', 'I think that he is creative because...' Now take each of these elements in turn and ask yourself how you know this. How does this person *demonstrate* each attribute? For example, if one of your words is 'flexible', think about how that can be broken down into smaller units. What does flexibility 'look' like? Do this for as many of your ideas as possible so that you are refining them into smaller and smaller constituents. Whenever you find yourself using a word or phrase that denotes a negative, such as 'not', 'never' or 'doesn't', look for a positive alternative. For example, if 'flexibility' includes 'doesn't get hung up on details' then you might change this to 'sees the bigger picture'.

Jo would like to be more creative in her approach to working with children. Her pyramid was based around a friend whom she considered to be a creative cook. She identified 'not worried

*about making mistakes' as one of the components of her view of
creativity. When encouraged to turn this into a positive statement
'not worried about' became 'relaxed about' and 'able to learn
from mistakes'. Now she had something that she could elaborate
on more fully.*

STORY-TELLING AND PUPPETRY ADAPTATION
See Story-building activity 6.3: Exploring structure.

Looking at the smaller elements of a concept not only gives us insight
into how we or others view that concept but can also suggest a starting
point for supportive interventions. It helps us to see the extent to which
we are already embracing the essence of that concept and helps us to
identify areas we might want to develop further.

Life circumstances may sometimes stifle creativity and it is not always
easy to recognise our own creative potential, but remember creativity is
not about producing great works of art. Everyone has the capacity to
imagine and everyone has the capacity to be creative.

Perhaps these first few exploratory activities have highlighted some
strengths and challenges for you. Maybe you also have some memories
or feelings sitting with you that you didn't have when you started to
read this book. You might like to jot down some of these as well. Try
to be accepting of any uncomfortable feelings as well as the joyful ones.
Remember, the aim of all these exercises is to help you to identify down-
to-earth principles and activities for interacting with children in a creative
and enabling way.

References

Dalton, P. and Dunnett, G. (2005) *A Psychology for Living: Personal Construct Theory for
Professionals and Clients* (2nd edition). Chichester: John Wiley and Sons.

Hillman, J. (1983) *Healing Fiction*. Connecticut: Spring Publications.

Kelly, G. A. (1955) *The Psychology of Personal Constructs*. New York: Norton.

Plummer, D. (2010) *Helping Children to Cope with Change, Stress and Anxiety*. London and
Philadelphia: Jessica Kingsley Publishers.

CHAPTER 5

Image-Making

*Following the stretching exercise that Morag had done with Jo
(see pages 36–37) she later drew a cat to represent how she
felt after playing a calming and focusing game that involved
listening to different sounds in the environment. Jo suggested to
Morag that she could pretend to be the cat for a few moments
and get a sense of what that felt like. Morag told Jo that she (the
cat) was sitting in the sunshine and felt warm and calm. Jo later
used this image as a helpful link for Morag to regain the same
feeling when she was thinking about facing a more challenging
situation ('Do you remember the feeling that you had when you
were imagining a cat? Imagine yourself being that cat now and
feel what that is like').*

Images are a natural part of our lives and are our earliest means of making
sense of the world. They form the basis of our knowledge about ourselves,
others and our environment long before we are ever able to communicate
through words.

As you read through this book you will be creating conscious and
unconscious[4] images of Ardan, Aisha, Morag and Ben. These images will
be influenced not only by what you have been reading but also by your
previous experiences. They will therefore reflect your uniquely personal

---

4   As Rollo May notes in his iconic book *The Courage to Create*, there is of course no such thing as *the*
    unconscious: '…it is, rather, unconscious dimensions (or aspects or sources) of experience. I define this
    unconscious as *the potentialities for awareness or action which the individual cannot or will not actualize*' (May,
    1975, p.55). Unconscious processes are of course multiple and complex but it is the positive aspect to these
    'potentialities' that is particularly relevant to the use of imagination in the context of this book.

understanding of the children. This is referred to as being influenced by our own *phenomenal field*. Even if two people have the same image it will undoubtedly be *experienced* in different ways and will mean something different to each person.

EXPLORATORY ACTIVITY 5.1: PHENOMENAL FIELDS

You will have noticed that the introductions to Ben, Morag, Aisha and Ardan differed in the amount of information given. Did this affect your initial impressions of each of them in any way? To what extent do you think your previous or current experiences influenced your connections with each of the children? Did one child's situation resonate more deeply with you than the others? Be aware of how your perceptions, memories and imagination could influence your engagement with each child's story.

STORY-TELLING AND PUPPETRY ADAPTATION

This is an interesting topic for discussion with older children when exploring story and puppet characters. Which character did each child warm to? Which one, if any, did they find it hard to engage with? Why was this?

EXPLORATORY ACTIVITY 5.2: IMAGES AND MODALITIES

Images may not necessarily be visual. For example, you might be able to *hear* Ardan speaking in your imagination, *picture* him seated in front of you and have a *sense* of his feelings and concerns, just from the descriptions already given.

What is the strongest image for you when you think of newly mown grass or freshly made bread? What images come to mind when you think of your favourite place to be?

Imagine yourself cutting into a fresh lemon. Do you imagine the smell of the lemon juice? Do you get a sense of the texture or the colour of the lemon? Do you perhaps have a physical response, such as a rush of saliva?

GENERAL ADAPTATION

With children you might talk about the various types of images: 'Some are like pictures, some are sounds (like imagining a conversation or a tune in your head), some are feeling or sensation images (like imagining the feel of velvet or mud or imagining what it's like for your friend to feel sad)'.

Remembering and imagining

Neuro nugget

The hippocampus, located in the temporal lobe of the brain, is involved in learning new information and is central to the formation of memories. Through its close connections with the amygdala, it plays a central role in the relationship between memory and emotion, assigning emotional 'value' to all our experiences (Nunn, Hanstock and Lask, 2008). Research indicates that the hippocampus is not just involved in remembering the past, but it also seems to be involved in imagining the future, presenting distinct differences in neuronal activity when we are undertaking these two different tasks (Kirwan, Ashby and Nash, 2014).

Researchers are continuing to investigate the links between imagining future events and remembering the past. What we can say just from experience though is that imagining yourself doing something can seem much more real than just *planning* to do something – images can be so powerful that we can have the same emotional and physical reactions to them as if they were actually present. Telling myself to sweat or to increase my heart rate will have little effect, but if I imagine a stressful future event vividly enough my body will respond as if that event were already happening. This can work in a positive direction too.

Neuro nugget

There have been many studies highlighting the positive benefits of using images to effect changes in the body. Neuroscientist Dr Shanida Nataraja highlights how such changes are, for example, evident when a person is meditating with an image in mind:

> The increased activity in the visual association area of the occipital lobe…acts to stimulate the hippocampus…conveying the sense of the emotional significance of the experience, as well as imprinting the experience in long-term memory… The hippocampus in turn stimulates the amygdala, which strengthens the emotional significance of the experience…
>
> The amygdala also activates the body's autonomic response through the midbrain. First the relaxation system is maximally activated, giving rise to a sense of blissful peace, and then the arousal system is switched on, giving rise to a sense of alert clarity of mind. (Nataraja, 2008, p.92)

Carl Jung believed that imagination does not rely on memory and current perceptions alone:

> Completely new thoughts and creative ideas can present themselves from the unconscious – thoughts that have never been conscious before. They grow up from the dark depths of the mind like a lotus and form a most important part of the subliminal psyche. (Jung, 1978, p.25)

Image-making can be a useful and safe way to aid this flow of 'new thoughts and creative ideas', which are so often the spur for change. In this instance we are facilitating those moments of realisation that help children to move forward with their understanding of themselves and with their aspirations. So, for example, if I ask you to allow an image to emerge that somehow represents how you are feeling right now, each reader will of course see, hear or sense something different. I have done this activity many times when I write and every time I do it I have a different image.

For example, this time an image of a cardboard box comes to my mind! My initial reaction to this is one of curiosity – I wonder what is inside. But when I open it up the box is empty. I am disappointed. In my imagination I ask the box a little angrily, 'What's so good about being you?' 'Ah!' says the box, 'I am waiting to see what you will make out of me!' If a box could show a 'wry smile' then that is what this one would do! I realise that this relates to what I have just been writing about creative ideas – and that has given me an idea for a story!

IMAGE-MAKING GUIDELINE 5.1:
IMAGES DO NOT REQUIRE INTERPRETATION

Although we may have ideas about what a child's images represent, we should avoid simplistic interpretations. If you keep an open mind and approach the exploration of images with great respect you will help the child to come to his own understanding. It is his perspective that is crucial and he may have completely different thoughts about the image to those that leap to mind for you. His understanding of an image may also remain below his conscious awareness. An image can 'do its work' without any need for interpretation, even by the explorer. Hillman (1990) reminds us that this is 'an imagination service, not an information service'. He suggests that we do not need to interpret the images that arise but that the image itself is more important, more inclusive and more complex than what we have to say about it. We need the image, not the explanation, to help us on our path.

IMAGE-MAKING GUIDELINE 5.2: IMAGES CAN LEAD TO
NATURAL CHANGE WITHOUT ADULT INTERVENTION

Treating a child's image-making with respect can sometimes involve waiting silently for a child to work through a difficult idea, perhaps just giving non-verbal signs of support such as a slight head nod or an encouraging smile while he draws or describes an image or while he plays with a toy that is indicative of an image. Giving children the opportunity to experience 'doing the work' for themselves will nurture their natural drive to change and grow.

IMAGE-MAKING ACTIVITY 5.1: EMOTION IMAGES

Focus your thoughts on one of the four children for a moment. Perhaps read through the introduction to this child again (Chapter 2). What is the strongest emotion that comes to mind in relation to this child? This could be an emotion that you imagine the child might be experiencing, or it could be your own emotion when you read about him or her.

Allow an image to come to mind that somehow represents this emotion. For example, it might be an image of an object, an animal, a colour or a plant. Whatever image comes to mind, simply allow it to emerge, knowing that there is no wrong or right way of doing this. Make a note of the image or sketch it so that you can refer back to it later.

Adults may sometimes assume the presence of more complex emotions in children than they are actually capable of. In contrast, it is also possible that we can underestimate the depth of feeling experienced by some children just because they don't yet have the vocabulary to describe them. Images bypass this complexity and can help us towards a greater understanding of how a child feels.

Let's go back to Morag and her game of musical chairs. She may or may not be aware of her emotions but Jo does not have the chance to explore this aspect with her until later when Morag and the other children are busy drawing pictures and writing about the games they have been playing. Jo squats down next to her so they are at the same eye level. There are just a few indiscernible words on Morag's paper.

Jo: Hello Morag.

(Morag moves her seat a little further away. Jo also adjusts her position to give slightly more space, noting that Morag is perhaps more comfortable with a greater distance from others than are the rest of the children in the group. Jo finds herself wondering

why this might be but immediately brings her focus of attention back to the present moment and to Morag.)

Jo: I can see you've written some things down already. Can you tell me about what you've written?

(Morag continues to stare at the paper.)

Jo: I wonder how you are feeling about the games right now?

Morag: (mumbles) I hate playing games.

Jo: Sometimes you really hate the games we're playing.

Morag: I don't want to play stupid games. I can't do them (kicks the table leg forcefully).

Jo: Some games are a bit hard and you get cross with me.

(Morag shakes her head).

Jo: Maybe you get cross with yourself?

(Morag nods).

Jo: Sometimes when I get cross I want to cry. Is that maybe what happened to you?

(Morag looks at Jo but does not say anything.)

Jo: (nods) Okay. I think I understand (pauses)… I wonder what we can do together to help with that cross feeling? (Morag shrugs) Mmm you're right – it's a tricky one. I'd like to help if I can. Let's see… When we're playing these games and you're not cross, how does that feel?

Morag: Dunno. Okay, I guess. Like the cat (referring to the earlier image representing calmness).

Jo: Sometimes you feel okay like the cat and sometimes you feel cross like…

Morag: A hissy snake!

Jo: Sometimes cross like a hissy snake. I wonder what that snake wants to say.

In working towards the use of images Jo demonstrated key elements of a 'perceptually intelligent', respectful dialogue with a child (see page 23). I have included as many points as possible in such a brief extract, yet on first reading it may seem quite straightforward. This highlights the importance of this type of interaction – the concept is simple and the benefits are numerous:

- Jo started by putting herself at a similar level to Morag physically. Wherever possible it helps the communication process if we can be on the same level as the child (not towering above them, asserting our authority!).

- Throughout the conversation she was aware of Morag's need for both physical and emotional boundaries.

- By being 'fully present' for Morag, Jo realised that she needed to put aside her thoughts about the wider issues that Morag is possibly facing. This could be something that she needs to talk over with her colleagues and perhaps with her supervisor. For now, she simply uses mindful listening to observe and interact with Morag in the moment.

- She used Morag's name right at the start of the interaction and gave eye contact even though Morag did not return this for some time.

- She heard and acknowledged the problem.

- She commented on Morag's paper rather than making any sort of judgement (positive or negative).

- She made a tentative suggestion about the cause of Morag's distress without going into too much detail and without trying to 'rescue' the situation by giving advice or reassurance.

- She used non-judgemental words like 'tricky'.

- She demonstrated the 'normality' of feelings.

- She used the word 'cross' rather than 'frustrated' because she was aiming to match Morag's level of vocabulary with regard to emotions. Different degrees of emotion will be something that the group will be exploring at another time. Frustration can be introduced when they talk about the different nature of angry feelings from mild irritation all the way up to being furious.

- Jo also introduced the possibility for change by using words such as 'sometimes' and by looking for the exception to the feeling of being cross.

- She kept her expectations realistic. Morag will not be able to change her feelings of frustration overnight but she can begin to make small changes and Jo's words reflect this belief in her. She takes the approach of an interested co-explorer: 'I wonder what this snake is telling us' and 'If this cat could talk, I wonder what it would say.'

- She has opened up an avenue for the further exploration of feelings via the medium of images, beginning tentatively to help Morag to extend her images beyond the cat, which she has used before. She may encourage Morag to draw the images or Morag might feel comfortable talking about them or making up a story about how the cat and the snake interact.

The way in which a child connects with his images will most likely be a reflection of his current coping mechanisms. If Morag's cat suddenly grows wings and takes her on an adventure then that might indicate to Jo something about how she is coping with the activity that they are doing or how she is coping with the stressful situation she is facing at home. Jo might make a mental note to revisit that at another time, but for now, she would just need to acknowledge the transformation. This is one of the major advantages of working through play and imagery – we can help a child to see alternatives without negating their current ways of coping with life's difficulties.

Suggesting an image

There will be occasions when you are so in tune with a child's concerns and dilemmas that you spontaneously have an image that just seems to fit. Taking the opportunity to share this image with a child has two advantages. First, it demonstrates the normality and value of this way of thinking. Second, it may well trigger a deeper insight for the child.

When Aisha is faced with a difficult situation, Laura might have an intuitive sense of what the problem feels like for her daughter. She might share this in the form of an image: 'This problem feels like a muddy puddle. I wonder what we could do.' As I was writing that, I had an image of Aisha splashing around in the mud and having fun with the 'problem' but the situation may be far too serious for her to contemplate play in this way. Instead, it may be one that requires careful negotiation across the mud or around it to avoid being splashed at all costs. Or perhaps it is a problem that calls for a different image altogether – 'Yesterday's problem was like a muddy puddle but this one feels different. How does it seem to you?'

EXPLORATORY ACTIVITY 5.3: LIFE PATHS

Image-making activities can be as complex or as simple as a child needs and can cope with. Let's look now at a lengthier activity based around a 'life path'. Life-path exercises are sometimes used in therapeutic and teaching work as a way to facilitate a review of important people, events and circumstances in a person's life. The explorer usually starts from birth or a key event in childhood and works towards the present moment. In the following activity you will approach the task slightly differently, tracing a path backwards from the present moment. You will need your notebook or a large sheet of paper and some coloured crayons or a pencil. Since it is often easier to allow images to emerge when we have our eyes closed, you might like to have someone read the instructions to you. Otherwise,

I suggest that you read these a couple of times and then give yourself plenty of time to explore the path and to draw or write about your images.

Settle yourself in a comfortable position and close your eyes. Imagine yourself standing at a point on a path that stretches ahead of you and behind you. This point represents the present moment. Allow an image to come into your mind that somehow represents how you feel at this moment in relation to your caring role. This image might be an object, a person, a colour, a plant or an animal, or it might be a word – anything at all that somehow represents how you feel. When an image comes to mind open your eyes and draw it or write about it.

Close your eyes again. Imagine yourself turning to look back along the path at the journey you have already made. You may want to imagine an aerial view. Take some time just to get a feel for the type of path that you have been following. Is it mostly rocky or mostly smooth? Perhaps it is hilly or flat, or a mixture of both. What can you see on the path? What can you see at the sides of the path?

Now look back to a point on the path that represents a relatively recent time – say two months ago – what was happening at that point? When you feel that you have a sense of what was happening two months ago, take a longer view, perhaps six months, or even a year. Keep doing this until you have identified several points along the path that you feel have influenced your current decisions and attitudes.

When you are ready, open your eyes and bring yourself fully back to the room. You might do this by moving your feet in order to feel the solidity of the floor or simply shift your position and have a stretch. When you feel fully present within the room draw or write about your path. Please do this before you talk to anyone about it.

Thinking about a life path, with specific emphasis on what has influenced your current choices, can be illuminating in itself and you may not feel the need to explore this any further. If you *do* want to think about it in more depth however, here are some of the questions that I have found helpful.

- How much did I feel in control of the choices that I have made so far?

- At any point, did I have other choices, other paths that I could take?

- What factors influenced my choice of this particular path at each significant point?

- How much do I feel in control of the way in which I proceed along the path into the future?

- Have I pictured myself alone on the path or were there any key helpers or mentors for me along the way? How might I draw on my own strengths and on the help of others in the future?

- How does this path interrelate with the paths of significant people in my life (e.g. my parents, my child, my partner)?

- Am I aware of the factors contributing to any noticeably smooth or rough areas of the path? For example, was it smooth/rough because of outside influences, because of my own attitude/emotions or due to a combination of factors? How might this inform my future choices?

Mel and Greg explored this activity together. Mel drew a path full of rocks and deep holes. At her 'current position' she drew two figures to represent herself and Greg and wrote 'sad', 'angry' and 'exhausted' above their heads. At a point on the path that represented one month before this she added a very large rock. Three months before that she showed herself and Greg faced

> *with an even bigger boulder. She then added footsteps weaving backwards and forwards along the path. Mel reviewed her drawing at this stage and commented that it looked 'a mess' because of all the footsteps. Greg suggested that Mel could add something surprising to the drawing and Mel immediately added a gate across the path just prior to the present point with a sign that said 'No Entry'.*

Life-path images are not always clear or obvious metaphors but they can be a useful starting point for further exploration and can lead to important moments of insight.

Once again, the image of Mel's path may have triggered many different thoughts in your own mind about meanings and possible support strategies. For example, although the past has clearly influenced her current feelings and decisions, the gate perhaps indicates that going back over old ground is not something that she wants to do at present. Our intuitions may or may not be on the right lines, however, and the only way to check this out would be to help Mel to come to her personal understanding and conclusions about what to do next.

If Mel did the life-path activity again in the future, she may find that some aspects have changed, perhaps without her conscious awareness.

IMAGE-MAKING GUIDELINE 5.3:
IMAGES CAN BE FLUID ENTITIES

Images that arise from outside our conscious awareness in this way are representative snapshots of how we experience ourselves and the world at that moment in time. They are not fixed entities. They can change quite naturally or we can consciously change them in order to influence positively our thought patterns and behaviours.

> *Ardan visualised his past experiences of stammering as a long road, full of treacherous holes and traps, with wild animals waiting to jump out of hiding places to pounce on him. When Ardan imagined himself walking along the road he realised that*

it had been trying to get him to where he wanted to go, but the journey was so full of fear that it was a slow and painful process.

During the course of his therapy Ardan was gradually able to note smoother areas on the path and to enjoy these without the constant fear of being caught in a trap at any moment. He learnt that he could control the wild animals to some extent so that they would not be completely unpredictable and unmanageable and would not fill him with so much fear when they did appear. Although Tom gradually encouraged Ardan to negotiate some of the holes and traps, rather than avoid them (avoidance often feeds fear), there were some potential 'dangers', such as giving a presentation in class and also ordering takeaways, which Ardan felt ill-equipped to face and which he therefore avoided assiduously. He needed some practical strategies and techniques to help him to deal with these situations in real life and this became the focus of his therapy.

Ardan was able to connect with the personal meaning of his imagery with ease. He quickly recognised that, because of his fear of stammering, any communication seemed fraught with dangers. By talking about this through the medium of images however, he was able to stay one step removed from the uncomfortable feelings, as if he were a story-teller. Tom encouraged Ardan to see the potential for taming the moments of stammering and negotiating his way through difficult experiences. Ardan, in effect, constructed a more useful set of images that could potentially lead to actual reduction in fear of stammering.

GENERAL ADAPTATION

For a general adaptation of the life paths exercise see page 111.

Summary

Making our innate capacity for image-making more conscious helps us to understand ourselves and others more fully. It also helps us to relate to children in a way that minimises many of the complexities of adult language and is closer to a child's own way of making sense of the world. It offers us a vehicle by which we can try to understand the world from the child's perspective and it gives children another way of expressing feelings and thoughts.

There are many ways in which the rich world of imagery can be extended into story-telling. In essence, a story is a carefully assembled collage of images and therefore all the guidelines for image-making will apply to story-making too. Here is a reminder of the first three image-making guidelines.

- Images (and stories) do not require interpretation.

- Images (and stories) can lead to natural change without adult intervention.

- Images (and stories) can be fluid entities.

The twelve principles suggested in Chapter 3 can all be creatively realised through image-making, story-telling and puppetry too. Understanding a child's imaginal world can help us to respond to individual needs in ways that respect each child's ways of thinking. Providing clear and consistent boundaries to indicate the shift from the child's life situations to the world of imagination and back again can help with the building of a trusting relationship and an interaction that 'contains' any difficult feelings or circumstances that a child might be facing. Manipulation of puppets and being a story-teller are safe and fun ways for children to feel engaged in the communication process without feeling pressurised. Opportunities for entering into the communication are boundless. Puppets can be verbose or non-verbal if necessary. Stories can be acted out, can prompt questions and can inspire other stories; they can be as short as a word or two and as lengthy as time and a child's enthusiasm allow. And appreciation of a child's story shared or a puppet that has managed to solve a difficult problem – well, that can be as short or as detailed as a child needs too!

References

Kirwan, C. B., Ashby, S. R. and Nash M. I. (2014) 'Remembering and imagining differentially engage the hippocampus: A multivariate fMRI investigation.' *Cognitive Neuroscience 5*, 3–4.

Hillman, J. (1990) 'Imaginal Practice.' In T. Moore (ed.) *The Essential James Hillman: A Blue Fire*. London: Routledge.

Jung, C.G. (1978) (ed.) *Man and His Symbols*. London: Pan Books (Picador edition).

May, R. (1975) *The Courage to Create*. New York: W.W. Norton and Company.

Nataraja, S. (2008) *The Blissful Brain: Neuroscience and Proof of the Power of Meditation*. London: Gaia, Octopus Publishing Group Ltd.

Nunn, K., Hanstock, T. and Lask, B. (2008) *Who's Who of the Brain*. London and Philadelphia: Jessica Kingsley Publishers.

CHAPTER 6

Oral Story-Telling

Ben sat silently on the carpet, a little removed from the other children. He stroked the owl puppet gently. He appeared to be totally focused on the story – it was very familiar to him and very repetitive. He knew exactly what was coming next. This was the first time that he had been calm all morning.

Engaging with oral story-telling on a regular basis encourages the development of self-calming, listening and focusing skills. Children like Ben, for example, who usually find it difficult to engage in the learning process, may sit for lengthy periods of time absorbed by the rhythm and content of an appropriately chosen story, where they may have previously been distractible or anxious during other tasks.

 Neuro nugget

One of the primary developmental tasks in the emotional life of a young child is the establishment of an effective emotion-regulation system: the ability to self-regulate and self-calm so that she is not constantly overwhelmed with difficult emotions.

There are two areas of the brain that are particularly important in the development of this self-regulatory capacity: the amygdala and the pre-frontal cortex.

The amygdala has been shown to be involved in the laying down of immediate and long-lasting emotional memories associated with perceived threat. For example, when a person or object is associated (even by chance) with a traumatic event, the amygdala will produce such a strong neuronal response that a future encounter with that same person or object will trigger the stress response regardless of any actual threat being present (Nunn, Hanstock and Lask, 2008).

The amygdala's primitive and rapid response to threat is, however, mediated by other areas of the brain, for example the pre-frontal cortex, which deals with feelings and social interactions.

When the system is working well, impulsive reactions to perceived threat can be inhibited or regulated via the 'thinking' processes carried out at this higher level, thereby preventing us from being overwhelmed, for example, by inappropriate fear and anxiety.

Without a well-developed pre-frontal cortex, children will not only have difficulty with self-control and self-regulation but also with the ability to feel 'connected' to others. This area of the brain is most vulnerable to outside influences during its critical period of development in the first four years of life. Such influences include the ability of parents to tune into their child's feelings and provide the comfort and positive touch that allow the emotion-regulation system to develop and to function effectively (Gerhardt, 2004).

We know that the benefits of telling stories go even deeper than helping children to self-calm and to focus. As with the image-making described in the previous chapter, the imagery to be found in stories will often capture a child's imagination and engage her emotions much more readily than language-based thought (Bornstein, 1988). Through stories, children have the opportunity to *imagine* life and to learn that our imagination affects the way that we experience and influence our environment and the events and relationships that we encounter.

EXPLORATORY ACTIVITY 6.1: TRADITIONAL TALES

Make a list of five or six fairy tales, myths or legends that you remember from your own childhood or have come across in adulthood. Do you generally remember the stories in detail or do you remember just a few key events and outcomes? Can you link a strong emotion to any of the tales? For instance, are any of the stories based on overcoming fear or on coping with sadness?

Through stories children can learn about differing perspectives, problem-solving and creative solutions to difficult dilemmas. Perhaps a story will resonate with events and circumstances in their own lives and offer insights about how to cope with these. Perhaps a favourite story is far removed from a child's everyday experiences but can nevertheless offer glimpses of possibilities and hope. The act of listening to and telling stories engages the imagination at a heartfelt level. This is particularly evident in traditional fairy stories. Rudolf Meyer writes of the profound nature of symbolism within fairy stories, which:

> told and retold by mother to child enrich those depths of soul from which our later hopes and ideals are born. Millions of human souls absorb the fairy-tale motifs during their formative years, and their feelings are given a direction which influences the whole character of a people. No other literary creation, not even the most lofty classical work, has such a fundamental effect on generations of people. (Meyer, 1997, p.10)

Fairy tales, folk tales, myths and legends are wonderful sources of comfort and wisdom for children and adults alike but story-telling does not need to be limited to traditional tales alone. Your own life experiences and skills mean that you can be both a teller of carefully chosen traditional tales and a teller of individually tailored stories that will help children to make sense of their world and help to promote well-being. We all tell stories when we tell our family, friends or colleagues about something that has happened to us, we have seen on TV or we have read about. It is not such a big leap from this to telling stories to children about made-up events and characters.

EXPLORATORY ACTIVITY 6.2: STORY MEMORIES

Your previous experiences of listening to and of telling stories are likely to affect how you relate to story-telling now.

What is your earliest, pleasurable memory of hearing stories? Take a moment or two to recall your experiences of someone telling you a story. This might have been within your family or it could have been at school or while you were on holiday for example. What is the strongest element of this memory? Is it the theme of the story/stories? Or is it the feelings that you had when listening to stories generally? Perhaps it is the story-teller that had the most impact, or the environment and circumstances in which the story was told. Was the story read to you or was it apparently 'made up' by the narrator?

Write down a few thoughts about your remembered experience or sketch the remembered scene. Try to flesh this out with as much detail as possible. Even if your early memories are a bit hazy, drawing or writing about it will help you to find the essence of the pleasurable nature of the experience.

GENERAL ADAPTATION

Exploring the pleasurable nature of stories and puppetry with children is an obvious adaptation of this activity. This can be done in general terms: 'Does anyone have a favourite story?' or more specifically: 'What made that particular story special for you?'

Experience and age

A child's previous experiences of listening to and telling stories are more important than chronological age when it comes to choosing something appropriate. Keeping this in mind, let's look at some very general guidelines for the type of stories that might appeal to Ben, Aisha, Morag and Arden.

Ben

Ben's memory ability will mean that short stories (around three to five minutes) will be most likely to hold his attention. For a short, simple story he is able to cope with several repetitions of a single idea. He also enjoys elements of 'call and response' (think of the classic call and response evident in pantomimes such as 'Where is that cat?', 'He's behind you!'). Rhymes and 'silly' humour can both be used to hold his attention. However, he has difficulties understanding concepts that are outside his personal experience and cannot yet tolerate too much ambiguity. For example, although he can cope with the idea of animals talking to each other when he plays with his farm, a tree that walks would be a more difficult concept for him. The following story, constructed by Ben's mother, is based on his current interest in farm animals and on a real need for the use of sunscreen. Ben was finding it difficult to tolerate having the cream. Mel used the small plastic animals from Ben's farm set to act out the story and invited Ben to add one choice of his own – a child of three or four will usually be able to contribute to a story and offer a simple story of her own, even if it consists of just a few words.

WHO BORROWED MY SUNSCREEN?

Once upon a time there lived a little lamb called Jake. Jake liked playing in the field with his brothers and sisters. In the winter time his woolly coat kept him warm but in the summer time the farmer took Jake's woolly coat away so that he could stay cool. When this happened Jake had to wear sunscreen so that he didn't get sore skin. One very hot day Jake wanted to go and play in the field but someone had borrowed his sunscreen. 'Oh no!' he thought, 'I don't have my woolly coat to stop me from getting sunburn. What shall I do?'

He asked the cow in the farmer's field, 'Have you borrowed my sunscreen?' The cow munched on some grass and looked at Jake like this ('chewing the cud'). 'No not me! I have thick skin to protect me from the sun. Why don't you ask the donkey?'

So Jake asked the donkey in the farmer's shed, 'Have you borrowed my sunscreen?' The donkey swished his tail and looked at Jake like this (make a 'sad' face) 'No not me!' he said very slowly. 'I stand in the shade when it gets too sunny. Ask the dog. He knows everything.'

So Jake asked the sheep dog in the yard, 'Have you borrowed my sunscreen? The sheepdog twitched his ears. He looked at Jake like this (make an appropriate face) and said... (wait for Ben to say 'No not me!') 'I have lots of hair to protect me from the sun. But I know who might have borrowed it.'

Who do you think Jake went to see next? (Use one contribution from Ben then finish with 'Go and ask the piglets.')

So then Jake asked the piglets in the pigsty and what do you know? The piglets all said, 'Yes it was me! Thank you! I get terrible sunburn.' And they gave the sunscreen back to Jake. 'Thank you,' said Jake, 'now I can go and play in the field' and he put on some sunscreen and gave some more to the piglets too. And now the farmer has got lots of sunscreen, enough for Jake and for the piglets too.

Ben loves visual humour and engages well with stories involving puppets. If Mel chose to tell a story on a more general theme of 'not liking something' then a bird that wrinkles its beak when asked if it likes worms or a lion that shivers and shakes and hides its head under its arm when it sees a bath, would perhaps be more effective than any words of protestation!

Morag

Morag is ready for stories that are full of magic and wonder, such as traditional fairy tales and fables. She is able to tell her own 'connected up' stories with a plot and an outcome and has started to add emotional elements to her story-telling. She is becoming more adept at thinking about cause and effect, not just for events but also the feelings involved.

She is able to cope with longer stories that can be continued over an extended period rather than at one encounter. She is also able to become more actively involved in the *process* of a story and reflect on the content in order to make predictions about what might happen next, make comparisons, draw conclusions and make judgements. When her curiosity is aroused by a story she will make creative connections, ask imaginative questions and actively seek solutions to story problems.

Aisha

Aisha is ready for myths and legends and stories about famous people overcoming adversities. She also enjoys stories about children who are a little older than herself and who will provide a role model for her. She can make up her own extended stories, dividing the plot into distinct chapters and following through a theme, possibly with a subplot too.

Ardan

Ardan is at a stage where he can reflect on the content of stories and can discuss the relevance of story content to his own life. He is likely to enjoy and benefit from historical and scientific stories and stories about different cultures. Stories reflecting struggles for independence, finding one's identity and establishing one's place in the world have all become important.

> Ardan and Tom discussed various famous people who had coped successfully with debilitating stammers. Ardan was interested to hear about them but did not warm to the idea of reading about any of them. He then began to talk about a book that he was reading 'for pleasure'. This was a story about a young explorer who had battled against prejudice and ridicule in order to join an expedition in search of medicinal plants. Ardan had felt inspired by the young man's persistence in the face of adversity. As he retold the story in his own words it became evident that there were certain qualities attributed to the explorer that Ardan had

already developed and that he could draw on to help with his own 'battles'.

The next activity is the first of 13 story-building activities. When combined together these will give you a solid structure for effective oral stories and will also form the basis for puppet plays.

STORY-BUILDING ACTIVITY 6.1: INITIAL THOUGHTS

Have a look at the notes that you made for Image-making activity 5.1 and Exploratory activities 6.1 and 6.2. With one of the four children in mind, jot down any further thoughts you now have in relation to how to structure a story for this child. Think also about the tone of the story and how you would like it to end – will there be a moral to the tale, a lesson learnt, a skill mastered? These are initial thoughts – try to keep them brief.

STORY-BUILDING ACTIVITY 6.2: THE SPIRIT OF A STORY

An easy and quick way to familiarise yourself with story structure is to get hold of some good-quality picture story books. You will quickly see that there are certain patterns that appear to work well. These can point you in the right direction for oral story-telling even if you are working with older children; the basic structure of a picture book can be seen in myths and legends too.

Choose a short picture book or children's novel. Read through it a couple of times then put it to one side. Ask yourself the following questions.

- What drew me to this story?
- Was it a familiar story or theme?
- Did the story engage me? Why was that?
- If I didn't engage with it, why was that?

- Was it a comfortable length or too long or too short?
- Did it have a 'satisfying' ending?
- Did it end with the resolution of a difficulty or with an element of hope?

The answers to these questions will give you an indication of those elements that constitute the 'spirit' of a story. I suggest that you try to find a traditional tale from two or more different cultures and go through the same process. Familiarise yourself with the ways in which traditional tales can reflect differing values, beliefs and ways of behaving.

STORY-BUILDING ACTIVITY 6.3: EXPLORING STRUCTURE

In Chapter 4 we explored one way in which we can break down a concept into its smaller constituents. We can use a similar activity for exploring story structure too.

Using the following questions as a guide, construct a pyramid diagram to show the component elements of the story (the heart). At each stage ask yourself: 'How does the author show/tell this?'

WHAT IS THE MAIN THEME?

Some common themes for stories are: life paths and going on a journey (see Exploratory activity 5.3 and Story-building activities 6.6 and 6.7); relationships and nurturing (see Chapter 9); building knowledge and confidence (see Chapter 10); achieving goals (Chapter 11); gaining mastery (Chapter 12). Do any of these feature in your chosen story? Is there more than one theme?

WHAT IS THE STORY PLOT?

The plot is the 'carrier' for the theme. It might centre on a task to complete, a problem to solve, a lesson to learn or perhaps a gift or an insight.

IS THERE MORE THAN ONE PLOT?

Simple stories with just one plot are the most effective for young children. Older children will cope with a main plot and one or more subplots.

HOW IS THE MAIN PLOT REALISED?

The answers to this question can be divided into character(s), action(s) and emotion(s).

CHARACTERS

How many characters appear in the story?

This will largely depend on the type of story. Most picture books and fairy stories will only have a handful of characters unless larger numbers can be easily remembered (such as the seven dwarves).

Who or what are the characters?

The main character (protagonist) will usually be a child or an animal but can sometimes be an adult. For example, humorous stories about forgetful or eccentric adults overcoming an obstacle or achieving a goal can provide a child with some sense of the normality of certain difficulties in life. There is also invariably at least one 'helper', a wise person or a role model. Often there is a trickster who tries to make the protagonist fail.

ACTIONS

It is helpful to view the action in three stages.

What happens at the start of the story? What happens in the middle? How does the story end?

Dividing a story into three parts will help you to remember the sequence of events. This is also helpful when you come to construct your own stories. For example, if the story features a task to complete, the three sections might be as follows.

- Beginning: introduce the main character(s) and describe the situation or state that will trigger the action. Specify the task to be completed.

- Middle: encounter the obstacle(s) that might prevent the task from being completed. Make two or more attempts to resolve the problem or overcome the obstacle(s), refining the strategy each time.

- End: Overcome the obstacle(s) and complete the task alone or with help. Bring the story to a believable close. Stories should always end with hope, even if it is not a happy-ever-after scenario.

Each of the three sections can be further developed by asking 'How does the action move along?' For example, are there any repetitive elements to the action? Many stories employ repetition as a way of helping children to engage with the theme. Three is a common number for major elements, such as three tasks to complete or three attempts to solve a problem.

Are there any noticeable 'bridging' phrases or moments of reflection between one major part of the action and the next?
For example, how is the transition from the beginning to the middle shown? How does the narrative move the reader/ listener from one task to another?

EMOTIONS
What is the main emotion in your chosen book?
How is this indicated? Is it specifically stated or do the words only hint at the primary emotion?
The emotional content is what makes a story come alive for both the listener and the teller.

Deconstructing a story in this way will help you to be creative with your delivery and with the development of new stories. The same component features are also relevant for puppet plays.

STORY-BUILDING ACTIVITY 6.4: HAVING A GO

Try telling the story that you have studied without looking at the book. You do not need to reproduce the story word for word. It will sound more natural and authentic if you tell it in your own way. Play with the structure, add gestures, emphasise different parts of the story (exaggeration is often a key element in oral story-telling). Play with animation and variety in your voice. Think about the pace of the story. Allow pauses, unless of course the story requires a speedy section! Notice the difference in your language use in comparison to reading a story aloud. Notice how spontaneous and inventive you can be with your delivery once you have the main outline in mind.

Using imagery to help with story structure

Let's now look at one way in which you might start to develop a central character for a story based on a quality that a child aspires to or a quality that she wants to develop further. You have already made a start with this when you looked at images to represent emotions (Image-making activity 5.1).

STORY-BUILDING ACTIVITY 6.5:
IMAGES AND CHARACTERS

Focus on one of the four children and get a feel for a trait or quality that he or she might be striving for or might benefit from exploring. Let's say that you feel 'self-belief' is an area of difficulty. Allow an image to come to mind that somehow represents self-belief in relation to the child. It might be an animal, an object, a person or a plant. Whatever it is, just allow it to emerge. When you have an image, make a note or a drawing of it. My immediate image of self-belief in relation to Morag is of a jelly baby sitting on a white horse and waving a colourful flag!

Now imagine that you can see life from the perspective of this image. What is the best thing about being this image? What is the worst thing? In my example of the jelly baby I might note that the best thing about being *this* jelly baby is my enthusiasm and good intentions but maybe the worst thing, or something that is not so good about being a jelly baby, is that, not only am I young, but I am made of jelly and I am therefore very vulnerable.

Now ask yourself: 'From the perspective of this image what do I need? What would I most like to happen?' Make a note of your thoughts in relation to your image.

This image could either become the main character in your story or could give an indication of how the story can be developed. Although I might not make up a story about a jelly baby, I could use the theme of a young protagonist accepting help (from the horse) in order to be able to 'ride to the rescue' of someone in need. In the story, I might relate self-belief to a realisation that helping in small ways can be important or that sharing responsibility is vital so that the young protagonist does not feel overwhelmed or worthless in the face of a difficult task. Remember, you are tuning in to the child first so that your image will be appropriate for him or her. I would have a very different image for self-belief for Ardan or for Aisha. Once again, there is no right or wrong way of doing this. You are simply exploring possible ways of building an appropriate story. If an image doesn't feel quite right, there will be a reason for this uncomfortable feeling. If this is the case, make a note of your image and then put it to one side. For now, it will have served its purpose as an illustration of image-making and may perhaps trigger a different story at a later time.

STORY-BUILDING ACTIVITY 6.6: A PROTAGONIST'S STORY PATH

Exploratory activity 5.3: Life paths is a very versatile tool. For example, once you have an idea for a story, imagine yourself as the main protagonist on his or her life path. In your imagination, start from your 'end point' in the story (when the dilemma has been resolved, the problem solved, the skill mastered, etc.). What is the main feeling that you (the protagonist) have right now? Look back along the path. How did you get here? What attitudes and intentions got you to this point? What happened along the way?

STORY-BUILDING ACTIVITY 6.7: MORE IDEAS

Life-path themes and 'journeying' are the basis of many traditional tales. The following are just a few ideas that you could explore in your story-telling within this theme:

- travelling to a new place and learning something about oneself on the way
- finding one's place in life
- making life choices
- meeting guides and mentors along the path
- exploring and appreciating cultural differences (different paths).

Look back at your notes for Exploratory activities 6.1 and 6.2 and Story-building activities 6.1–6.6. Do these now trigger any ideas for stories?

STORY-BUILDING ACTIVITY 6.8:
THE LANGUAGE OF STORIES

Story-tellers often use devices that indicate to the listener that they are now in a different realm to current everyday life. While the story protagonists are still facing dilemmas and decisions, life tasks and difficult relationships, they are somehow different – they lived 'long ago in a far-away place' or 'in a tiny hole in a tiny tree'; they are princes and princesses; they are talking animals; they have magical powers. In whatever way you want to tell your own stories, try to start with a few words that indicate this movement into the realm of imagination. Once you have set the tone for the story, remember to keep your wording congruent. If it was long ago and far away, don't bring in events and items that could only be relevant today.

Another way to start stories is to use sentences and phrases that provide tension or uncertainty or those that will grab the listener's attention: 'Everything in Mike's house was always in the wrong place', 'It was a very unusual Saturday', 'Have you ever heard a tortoise singing?'

Pointers

There are a few practical considerations that can contribute to the effectiveness of an oral story.

STORY POINTER 6.1

It is a good idea to have a strategy in mind for times when a child is finding it difficult to engage with a story and where you feel that this is directly affecting others in a group. If possible, try to maintain the magic of the story by remaining in character as your puppet or as the story-teller. For example, you might have one of your characters pause in the flow of the story to speak directly to the child in order to gain her attention.

STORY POINTER 6.2

Try to make a 'cosy' atmosphere. At home, your child might like to curl up next to you for a story. If you are telling a story to a group, bring them as close as possible so that you don't need to project your voice to the back of a room. Each child should feel as though you are speaking directly to her.

STORY POINTER 6.3

Use a designated story chair to signify the special nature of the event. Perhaps use a throw or a blanket to change the nature of the chair. To avoid unnecessary distractions, you could also have a screen behind the chair or place the chair in front of a plain wall.

STORY POINTER 6.4

Use a simple phrase that signifies the start of the story, such as 'Once in a far-away place'.

Don't feel that you have to explain everything that happens in your story. When the story finishes, stop!

STORY POINTER 6.5

Perhaps consider constructing a portable tool kit. You may find yourself in a situation where there is a restriction on storage space or you may be working in several different locations. A portable tool kit for creative activities can be invaluable in these circumstances. This might contain:

- coloured ribbon wound into a ball that can be thrown, rolled or unwound in group story-telling activities

- a large, soft cloth that can be used as a story shawl or to decorate a story-telling chair

- an unusual musical instrument or home-made noise-maker to start and end a story or to signal changes in a story or puppet scene

- coloured paper and crayons or pastels for children to draw elements of a story; paper to tear up for shadow puppets

- a talking stick or unusual object for turn-taking activities after completion of a puppet session or story

- scraps of material, cotton wool, elastic bands or a ball of string, lollipop sticks and pipe cleaners for making puppets

- modelling clay

- a few miniature figures.

In this chapter we have deconstructed the process of oral story-telling in order to identify the skeleton that holds it all together. However, before we go on to look at putting all these elements together again, let me take you back to Chapter 1 for a moment as a reminder that the real heart and spirit of a story emanates from our engagement with children in the 'in-between'. Once you have a feel for the processes of story-telling, the 'art' will become second nature. You can make a story as simple and as practical as 'Who borrowed my sunscreen?', as whimsical as a fairy story or as epic as a Greek myth. There will be times when you tell a specific story to fit a specific need (see Chapter 7) and times when you find yourself telling a story while you are out walking with your child, on a school trip, in the car or perhaps while you are working together on a project of some sort. These impromptu stories can open up all sorts of possibilities for discussion and can also stand alone as valuable experiences that don't require further discussion at all.

References

Bornstein, E. M. (1988) 'Therapeutic Storytelling.' In R. P. Zahourek (ed.) *Relaxation and Imagery: Tools for Therapeutic Communication and Intervention*. Philadelphia: W. B. Saunders.

Gerhardt, S. (2004) *Why Love Matters: How Affection Shapes a Baby's Brain*. London and New York: Routledge.

Meyer, R. (1997) *The Wisdom of Fairy Tales*. Edinburgh: Floris Books.

Nunn, K., Hanstock, T. and Lask, B. (2008) *Who's Who of the Brain*. London and Philadelphia: Jessica Kingsley Publishers.

CHAPTER 7

Making a Story for a Specific Need

Now you have all the basic elements of an oral story structure. Take some time to look back at your notes and drawings. As a reminder, you have some initial thoughts about themes and intentions for a story (Exploratory activity 6.2; Story-building activity 6.1). You have identified aspects of a story that might capture a child's attention (Story-building activity 6.2). With Story-building activities 6.3 and 6.4 you explored the structure of an effective story (theme, plot, characters, action, emotion). You have engaged in image-making to engender a possible protagonist (Story-building activity 6.5). You have explored an image to represent an emotion (Image-making activity 5.1). You also looked at the language of traditional tales (Story-building activity 6.8).

When you come to construct your stories it is useful to think about aspects of motivation touched on in Chapter 3. What is your motivation for telling this story? What is the motivation behind the actions and intentions of the characters in your story? What motivates your puppets to communicate? The life-path activities (Exploratory activity 5.3 and Story-building activity 6.6) have perhaps given you some ideas about how you can take your characters on a 'journey' from the beginning to the end of the story. Undoubtedly, there will have been thoughts that have occurred to you while doing some of the other activities too.

Having thought about all the elements separately, Story-building activity 7.1 demonstrates a method by which you can pull them together again using image-making. Let's first look at some notes that Laura made for a story for Aisha and then look at the method for arriving at these notes.

> *Aisha is anxious about entering an unfamiliar situation. She does not want to avoid this situation, but she does need some reassurance. Laura is aware that it is also important for Aisha to feel that she is making a positive contribution to solving her dilemma – in other words, that she can be the 'expert' in something. Laura makes the following notes as the basis for her first story.*
>
> * *Aisha's main feeling: Anxiety.*
> * *Image of anxiety: A small boat, very adventurous but one day it's caught in a storm at sea. Has never experienced this before. Buffeted in the wind.*
> * *The helper: A whale – big and strong and very steady in its course but not very adventurous.*
> * *Conversation: Whale says, 'I can keep you steady while you sail back to the shore but I have never been beyond this part of the sea and I don't know where to go.'*
> * *Resolution: How does the whale manage this? Tries to push the sailboat – doesn't work. Tries to carry the boat on its back – doesn't work. Swims alongside the boat and shelters it from the stormy waves. Little boat feels safe. Starts to tell the whale about different parts of the sea that it has sailed to and how beautiful they are. Promises to show the whale.*

STORY-BUILDING ACTIVITY 7.1: IMAGE-MAKING AND STORY CONTENT

As with previous image-making activities, you may want to ask someone to read these instructions to you:

* Bring to mind a child with whom you are working.
* Focus on one issue that is important for this child.

- What is the child's primary feeling that surrounds this issue?

- Close your eyes and relax. Allow an image to come to mind that somehow represents that feeling. It might be an animal, object or plant. Whatever it is, just let the image come.

- Explore the image in your imagination.

- Open your eyes and sketch or write a few notes about the image.

- Close your eyes again and relax.

- Allow an image to emerge that represents a 'helper' in this situation. Go with whatever comes to mind.

- Explore the *qualities* of this image.

- Open your eyes and sketch or write a few notes about this image.

- Now you have the bare bones of the *beginning* of your story.

- Close your eyes again and imagine a conversation between the two images. How can they help each other? What does the first image (the feeling image) need from the helper? What does the helper need from the feeling image? Allow the *middle* of your story to unfold.

- Open your eyes and put down a few notes or draw a picture to show the middle of the story.

- Relax, close your eyes and allow an image to emerge that represents a resolution to the situation or an understanding between the two images.

- When you are ready, open your eyes and sketch or write down the *end* of the story.

Now spend some time putting together the story, using all the ideas that you have from your notes. If possible, let this story sit with you for a day or two before you tell it to a child. Daydream about it but don't 'work' on it too much – just play with it!

Helping children to create their own stories

For some time after qualifying as a speech and language therapist I used colourful story books as an aid to my therapy practice with young children. Then one day a youngster rejected my offer of a book that had been a particular favourite of many children in the past. She told me that she had already seen the book at school and it was 'rubbish'. It clearly wasn't the right book or the right time for this book for her. I asked her if she had been shown any other books that appealed. 'No!' was her firm reply. 'Would you like to tell me a story about worries instead?' I asked. She jumped at the chance! The story that emerged was a very personal reflection of how she felt when she was worried and proved to be more meaningful for her than a ready-made story.

Once you feel comfortable with using image-making and story-telling you will undoubtedly find that the children who hear your stories are eager to have a go too! This should be encouraged and celebrated no matter how short or how complex these stories turn out to be (if they are consistently long-winded and rambling then a few gentle prompts to keep the story moving forward will usually suffice). Such stories don't need to be overtly therapeutic, although at some level they do often reflect the ways in which a child might be working through a difficulty or a new experience.

There may also be times when you want to encourage a child to construct a story for a very specific purpose, and in this instance there are some simple strategies and guidelines that can help to keep this a pleasurable and 'safe' activity. A story that a child tells in these circumstances might be one that will help him to work out a solution or resolution to a difficulty or to gain insight into a dilemma or an emotion. As with all the stories that *you* tell, such a story should always finish on a note of hope or positive completion. Your experiences of telling your own stories, your knowledge of the child and your abilities to be with him fully and with heightened perception will all contribute to a feeling of safety for him.

Guidelines for facilitating a story
Version 1

You will need several circles of paper and some pencils, crayons and pastels. The size of the circles should be the child's choice. Ensure that you have a mixture and at least three of each size. Some children will want the freedom to draw within large circles; others might prefer smaller, more contained circles for their drawings. For this activity children will need to understand the concept of 'opposite' and should also be familiar with the idea of 'beginning, middle and end'.

Ask the child to sit quietly for a few moments and 'tune in' to the difficulty – for example, what it feels like to be worried all the time or being anxious about a music test. This will be the theme of the story.

Ask him to close his eyes if he feels comfortable to do so. Some children will want to keep their eyes open. This is okay too.

Prompt him with an instruction such as: 'Let an image (or picture) come into your mind that somehow shows us what it is like to feel worried all the time/feel sad/be on the go all the time.'

Ask him to let you know when he has an image.

Allow him time to explore the image in his mind for a short while before he opens his eyes and draws it in the first circle.

Now ask him to take a second circle and draw the opposite of the first picture. It is important that this is a personal opposite, not one that has been provided for him. Give him plenty of time to draw the images. Sometimes a child will add something important just at the last minute.

Look at the two drawings together. Ask the child to tell you about the drawings, gently prompting him to expand on feelings and actions (see the following example for Aisha). Now start to expand the story: how does the first picture become the second one? Or, how does it move nearer to being *like* the second one? Gradually, a story will emerge. Elements of this story should then be drawn in a third circle and placed between the other two pictures so that the story is 'contained' and you can both see the progression.

Some ideas for prompt comments and questions

Aisha drew a single figure alone in a big boat on a stormy sea for her first picture. In the second picture the figure was with friends in a smaller sailboat on a calm sea.

Start with comments; leave plenty of pauses for responses. For the first picture I might say some of the following:

- You have drawn a person in a boat. It looks like a big boat.

- You have drawn very high waves. Do the waves make a noise?

- I wonder what that person feels like/is thinking.

- I wonder what it would be like to be that boat.

- If the boat could speak I wonder what it would say.

- What does the little girl/person want to say to the boat?

Note that I am not commenting on the quality of the picture, for example: 'What a great picture, well done, you're good at drawing', etc. The aim of my comments and (limited) questions is to flesh out the characters and the context ready for the story. Start with neutral words (e.g. person) unless, of course, the context is obvious (big boat, high waves). As soon as the child uses any specific words, change your own comments/questions accordingly. For example, if he tells you that it's a *little girl* then reflect this back to him.

When you both have a 'feel' for the elements of the characters within the story, move on to the second picture. Before doing so, I might first comment on the impact of the first picture: 'Thank you. Your picture really shows me what it must be like to be worried all the time. I understand much better now.'

Remember – avoid any temptation to interpret the pictures for the child. One such interpretation might go something like this: 'In this picture you are all alone in the boat. That must be scary. Having friends with you when things are difficult can really help a lot.' My belief is that the stories are more powerful and effective in doing their job when I can minimise my own thoughts about what the pictures mean to *me* and really listen to what they mean to the *child*. However, it naturally falls to facilitators to 'guide' or reassure children who are struggling to resolve problems and dilemmas, and so the story of how to get from picture A to picture B may need more structured but tentative prompting. For children who are reluctant to talk about their pictures, you will obviously have to rely much more on your own intuition.

Version 2

Some children may not want to draw, in which case you might use small figures from which they can choose a selection, or use real objects that are close to hand – children are very adept at making up stories with anything that they can find! I have a large story-telling box that contains many smaller boxes. In each of these smaller boxes there are collections of random or sometimes themed objects. For example, one has a family of miniature bears, one has a seaside theme and another has a collection of plastic 'gem' stones. I mostly use these as visual reminders for my own stories (see Story-building activity 13.1: Remembering a story) but they are also helpful for children who want to act out a story through play.

Giving feedback

When a child has completed his own story your feedback needs to be affirming and accepting. All the principles of praise and appreciation (pages 30–32) and the image-making guidelines (5.1–5.3) should be considered.

It can be particularly helpful to summarise the story for the child. This reinforces the fact that you heard it and took it seriously. It may also help him to process it further. With some children I have written the story out and attached their illustrations, making a special 'story book'. You might also consider making a digital presentation together so that you can embellish it with sound effects, music and animated pictures. I remember a child who took such a story to school for 'show and tell'. Anything that makes it 'special' for a child is worth taking time over.

Before looking at story-telling themes in more depth, the next chapter focuses on puppetry. Once you have the basics of puppetry under your belt, you will be able to transfer stories to this medium. Puppets are not only for story-telling though – they have many roles to play in the 'in-between'.

CHAPTER 8

Puppetry

Ardan was interested to learn that puppetry was not just for kids and that it had its origins in ancient times. He spent time researching shadow puppets and learnt that they were originally used to represent people's ancestors. The puppets would give messages and advice on family matters or in times of trouble. He made an intricate shadow puppet and demonstrated its use as part of a history project. He found that when he spoke as the puppet his speech was much more fluent and he enjoyed the liberation from the pressure he had experienced in previous presentations.

The ability to enter the world of a story as if it could really happen is also evident when children interact with puppets 'as if' they have a personality of their own. Puppets are very different to dolls. In traditional doll play, the doll might be manipulated by the child, who causes it to do certain things. Puppets, however, have their own 'personality', and therefore they connect with children in a different way. A child who manipulates puppets successfully knows that he is engaging with an audience; he is making connections with other people via the puppet, rather than being involved, for example, in solitary or parallel play. Similarly, being in the audience requires different levels of involvement, perhaps focused listening and observation, a suspension of judgement about the authenticity of the character, a direct involvement with the puppet as if it were alive. Have you ever watched children watching a puppet show? Are their eyes generally on the puppeteer or on the puppet?!

As with oral story-telling, puppetry also has a long tradition. For centuries, puppet theatre has been an important art form, reflecting deeply held aspects of Chinese, Indian, Indonesian, Japanese and Eastern European cultures. In the last 40 years the art of puppetry has also gained wider respect and recognition in Western Europe and in the United States. Many teachers and therapists are now using puppets as a way to enhance their work with children. What is it that makes puppetry such a valuable medium for interaction? In 1991 the Calouste Gulbenkian Foundation undertook an enquiry into puppetry in the United Kingdom and Ireland. The resultant book, titled *On the Brink of Belonging*, captures the essence of puppetry and the reasons for its universal appeal:

> Puppetry is, and has been since the earliest days of human existence, the investment of matter with spirit by human agency. Puppetry is the ability to give life to ideas…its edge is the fantastic. It is the ability to create meaning, to give purpose, and to offer intelligibility to different worlds… Puppet theatre contradicts our logic and liberates our imaginations. There is an ineffable sense of play, of the fantastic, of the surreal, of the 'always possible' of worlds we *could* inhabit. (Allen and Shaw, 1992, p.9)

This sounds very similar to the wonderful gifts that can be derived from story-telling and, of course, puppet plays are indeed just that – animated story-telling. As suggested at the end of Chapter 7, however, even if you are not intending to write plays for puppets, they can have an important role in building relationships and enabling change. Puppets can help quiet children to express themselves with more confidence. A puppet can embody emotions, impart pearls of wisdom, create opportunities for problem-solving, listen to children's hopes and troubles, provide comfort, offer insights into other people, act out fears and worries 'safely', express talents, be naughty, get told off…the possibilities for safe puppet play at home, at school and in a therapeutic environment are huge.

PUPPETRY POINTER 8.1: CHOOSING AND DEVELOPING PUPPET CHARACTERS

I admit that I am easily persuaded to buy 'characterful' puppets. I have a large collection now and they have been well loved by many children over the years. Most have been invaluable helpers in therapeutic environments and during story-telling activities. However, as my confidence grew in the use of puppets I learnt the incredible value of making puppets for specific uses and of engaging children in the process of creating their own animated protagonists. The emphasis here is on creating. In Story-building activity 6.5 you explored an image or images that represented character traits. In the same way that different images will reflect different characteristics, puppets can also be imbued with different qualities. This will primarily become apparent through the material used in its construction. A glove puppet, for example, moves in a very different way to a marionette (a puppet that is manipulated by strings) or a rod puppet. If you are just starting off with using puppets, try to get hold of three or four different types so that you can 'play' with them, see how they move and check out how you can show different personalities and different emotions. Which type of puppet do you feel most comfortable with?

Also think about the puppets that the children with whom you work will feel comfortable with. Try to get a feel for which type of puppet they will be happy to hold and manipulate. Which ones will be most likely to enhance their communication and self-expression?

Almost anything can be animated in order to express a unique character. Here are some home-made puppet ideas to try:

• Tie five knots in a square of silk (four corners and a head) and it becomes a 'sprite', a person or an animal. Different coloured squares will imbue the sprite with different energies. Adding a small pebble or coin into the knots will also change the nature of its movements. Tie lengths of cotton to the 'wrists' and 'ankles' of the puppet and loop the other end around your fingers. Now the puppet can dance, walk, sit or even fly onto a child's shoulder.

- Tear out paper shapes to make shadow puppets – the tearing, rather than cutting, allows for greater freedom of form and takes away the pressure of cutting things out accurately.

- Use wooden spoons or wooden spatulas as a basis for the body of a puppet. Large pieces of lightweight material that can be gathered around the 'neck' of the spoon as a dress or cloak, allowing for a flowing movement when the character walks. Heavier materials will give the character a different 'feel', perhaps more gravitas or maybe a more 'plodding' or even 'sad' movement.

- Use sock puppets for characters who will talk, make funny faces and generally engage in a humorous way with children. Use buttons and felt for faces. Oversized features (large eyes, a long, red tongue or a large button nose) accentuate the character of the puppet and help to emphasise different emotions. Having socks with 'opposite' characters (one for each hand) can be a fun way of exploring different characteristics, beliefs and behaviours. For example, red sock is a fiery character, always on the go; blue sock is a calm, quiet character, very 'laid back'. How will they each take on the difficult task of helping a friend who is being bullied? Can they work together to find a solution?

- Plastic or polystyrene cups or balls of various sizes threaded together can produce all sorts of bendy characters, allowing for flowing movements or ungainly movements perhaps.

- Use stretchy gloves to make a set of finger puppets. Cut the fingers off at the base for separate puppets or keep the glove whole for a larger puppet, perhaps one that has a head, arms and legs.

- Give a 'found' object a 'voice' and see what story it comes up with. A pencil could tell how it used to be part of a tree, how it was carefully crafted to make a useful tool, how it loves to help children learn how to form letters and so on. Visit second-hand shops and craft shops for various bits and pieces that might transform into puppets.

PUPPETRY POINTER 8.2: GETTING TO KNOW YOUR PUPPET

'Live' with your chosen or made puppet for a while before using it for the first time. Have imaginary conversations with it and find out about its character. Experiment with a 'voice'; the first voice you choose may be exactly right but often it emerges as your puppet's character develops. Rehearse your puppet's voices and try not to make them too squeaky – give them the voice that suits their character and gives them authenticity.

PUPPETRY POINTER 8.3: EXPANDING THE CHARACTER

'Hot seating' a puppet is a great way to expand on its character. Having made a puppet individually or as a small group exercise, participants give it a name and decide where it lives. The individual or group then sits with their puppet and invites questions from the 'audience'. Questions are directed to the puppet: 'What is it like to live there?', 'What is the best part of your life?', 'Who are your friends?' and so on. Of course, this doesn't need to be done as a group exercise. Individual children can sit with their own puppet on the hot seat or you can hot seat your puppet for children to ask questions.

PUPPETRY POINTER 8.4: MANIPULATING THE PUPPET

Puppets should appear to have a life of their own. One way of emphasising this is to make sure that you pause when the puppet moves. I have already mentioned how the weight of the materials used to make a puppet can help to portray different characters and moods. Specific movements can also be used to good effect. Puppet movements tend to be larger-than-life movements (but not so overdone that they take away from the authenticity of the character in the child's eyes). A slight raising of shoulders for a 'don't know' shrug for example might be missed – slightly overemphasise it and perhaps even mirror it – your puppet shrugs and you look at it and say 'Tell me more about that' (copying the shrug).

One of the times when you might not use overemphasised movements is if you are 'walking' a puppet in mid air across the space in front of you. It is better to glide the puppet across with a slight wave motion rather than 'bounce' it up and down. This gives a more believable sense of walking, unless of course your character is one that does actually move by jumping up and down!

Actions should be paced – don't have the puppets moving around all the time; match new actions to new ideas or thoughts.

If you are using two puppets, one in each hand, remember to carry on manipulating the second puppet while the first one is the main focus of attention. It is easy to 'forget' the other puppet so that it does not look at all engaged in the process. Keep it upright and 'present' for your audience. Perhaps it is listening to the first puppet or occasionally looking at the audience or nodding. Keep the speaker more active than the other characters but do not over do it!

Personal space needs to be bigger for puppets. They generally don't come into contact with each other. Keeping them apart prevents them from becoming 'objects'.

PUPPETRY POINTER 8.5: SCRIPTS FOR PUPPET PLAYS

There are many different ways of constructing a puppet show. For example, a puppet might be a story-teller, you and your audience might interact with a puppet directly or a child might be a story-teller and use the puppets to 'act' the story. The power of oral story-telling and puppet plays lies in the seeming spontaneity of the engagement with the audience. Both media are very different to reading a story from a book or reading the dialogue of a play out loud. For this reason, there is no need to overwrite a script for puppets. You might use an oral story for your basis but limit the characters involved and limit the number of scenes to three or four. Think about stage directions and remember that one of the main differences between oral story-telling and puppetry is that, for puppets, *showing* is more effective than *telling*. You will want to keep each character's speech to a minimum. Show feelings by gestures, whole-body movements and interactions between the puppets. For example, a shy or anxious tortoise withdrawing into its shell and shaking while a playful puppy jumps about in front of it is more effective than having the tortoise enter into an explanation of how it is feeling. Remember, we give many more non-verbal cues in our interactions than we are consciously aware of. Puppets can't always do this. Glove puppets with mouths can change their expressions to some extent (particularly sock puppets), but, in general, puppets show their intentions and emotions through whole-body movements.

Just as you might rehearse a story, rehearse the puppet play well before you show it to children. It can help to rehearse this in front of a mirror so that you can check that your puppets are in the right position for interacting with each other and with your audience. Also, practise entrances and exits so that you can keep your puppet in character from beginning to end. They will lose their potency if they just suddenly 'appear' or if they simply lie down or drop to your side on completion of the story.

PUPPETRY POINTER 8.6: WHEN A CHILD HAS DIFFICULTY ENGAGING WITH A PUPPET PLAY

If a child is absorbed in their own thoughts, is particularly anxious or excited or has a specific difficulty in focusing their attention, you may need to use simple prompts to indicate that you are initiating a conversation. For example, say her name first. Maintain eye contact but don't worry too much if she finds keeping eye contact with you difficult. In the same way, it may be necessary to use prompts throughout stories and plays. Make sure your puppets 'keep eye contact' with the audience. Imagine that you make a puppet and introduce it to a child or group with: 'This is Oliver Orang-utan.' Compare this with holding the puppet on your lap and orientating it so that it is looking at the audience. The puppet looks slowly around the group, then it looks at you and back to the group. It 'coughs'. You look directly at the puppet. The puppet moves its position slightly. Leaning forward and looking at a child in the front row it says, 'Hello I'm Oliver. What's your name?' The scene is set!

PUPPETRY POINTER 8.7: FOCUSING ATTENTION

I would encourage you as a puppeteer to look at your puppet frequently as if you were listening to it talk. If you look at children while your puppet is talking with them, they will tend to engage with you, not the puppet. When the puppet is listening to a child speak, however, you can *both* demonstrate active listening. Think about how you show a child that you are interested and listening fully. Practise ways in which your puppet can show this level of engagement with what a child is saying. *Repeating back can be very affirming.* Just as in person-centred counselling, occasionally repeating back or summarising what a child has said shows that you (or a puppet) have listened and understood or that you are at least *trying* to understand their perspective.

PUPPETRY POINTER 8.8: DISTRACTIONS

It is important to keep distractions to a minimum during both story-telling and puppet plays. Aim for a quiet environment without too many bright pictures, toys and so on in view. With puppet plays, avoid the use of too many props and staging – keep it simple. This said, for both stories and puppet plays you may want to signal the beginning of the performance with a short piece of appropriate music or by using a 'noise-maker'. I have a collection of noise-makers, which have proved very useful – an ocean drum for example or a thunder-maker can set the tone for a dramatic tale, a wooden flute or a gentle rainmaker would give a different feel.

PUPPETRY POINTER 8.9: ENDINGS

Practise 'finishing' a story. What will your puppet(s) do? If they go to sleep make sure that they face you in a sleeping position perhaps in the crook of your arm, otherwise they will still be staring at the audience! If they are going to walk away from the 'stage', try doing this slowly and have the puppet stop and wave to everyone or take a bow as it walks off.

When you have finished with a puppet please do treat it with 'respect'. It will have played an important role in a child's learning and in the building of a relationship. Do place it carefully face up or in a sleeping position on a chair or shelf or in the place that it is stored.

Now that you have dipped into the heart of stories and puppetry and you have explored the spirit that makes them work smoothly, I hope that you feel confident enough to make a start with story-telling and puppetry. I suggest that you look back at the story that you constructed earlier (pages 76–77) and begin to think of ways in which you would adapt this for a puppet play or for an interaction between a puppet and a child. Keep referring back to the guidelines given in this chapter. Think about the best type of puppet(s) for your particular story and how you would limit the dialogue and emphasise the actions. Write a short script with stage directions and practise your puppet's movements. Then give life to your ideas!

In the next three chapters we will look in more depth at some significant story themes for children of all ages and explore images and puppetry further. Once again, we will start from your personal perspective and also look at how Ardan, Aisha, Morag and Ben might reflect some of the ideas that we are exploring.

References

Allen, K. and Shaw, P. (1992) *On the Brink of Belonging. A National Enquiry into Puppetry.* London: Calouste Gulbenkian Foundation.

CHAPTER 9

Stories about Relationships and Nurturing

This theme is central to many stories and carries great importance for children and adults alike. If we are going to offer stories about nurturing, then it is vital that we understand our own views of this concept and how nurturing can take different forms at different times of a child's life.

EXPLORATORY ACTIVITY 9.1: NURTURING

Take two minutes to write down as many ideas as you can about the concept of nurturing. Try not to think about this too deeply – just write down your thoughts as quickly as you can. Keep going for the full two minutes. Try to fill the page. When you feel that you have run out of ideas add just one more!

All our past experiences and learning contribute to our understanding of what constitutes a supportive or nurturing relationship and this in turn will inform our telling of stories about nurturing, either tacitly or explicitly.

Our understanding of nurturing is initially based on our early life experiences with our primary caregivers. The degree to which our needs for nourishment and safety are met, we feel loved and are responded to with positive touch and positive language will have a long-lasting impact on our development and on our future relationships with others. We know that a healthy emotional attachment to principal caregivers is of prime importance in a child's emotional development. Positive, nurturing relationships help children to build emotional intelligence and resilience, paving the way for healthy self-esteem and the ability to form friendships, learn successfully and cope with life's ups and downs more easily.

Neuro nugget

Studies have shown that four-year-olds who have been brought up in highly stressful environments have a measurably smaller pre-frontal cortex compared with four-year-olds who have experienced a nurturing environment. These children show clear signs of lack of social competence, an inability to manage stress and the inability to see things from another child's viewpoint (Gerhardt, 2004).

Stories about nurturing (both nurturing of self and nurturing others) can be particularly helpful to children who are negotiating difficulties with their primary carers. Many of these children will reflect such difficulties in their encounters with other adults. They may want support but will react to offers of help in ways that seem to negate this. Some will want to push you away, either physically or verbally, others may be extremely defensive in asserting their independence and some will constantly demand your attention or be over compliant or withdrawn. Once again, knowing a child's background will always help us to understand a little more about his perspective and why he might think and behave in the ways that he does. We are then in a better position to be able to construct individually tailored nurturing stories.

Nurturing as a construct

As suggested in Chapter 4, we cannot automatically assume that a word we think of as denoting a particular experience will have the same meaning for everyone else. The word 'nurturing' is a good example of this – nurturing is a construct; it is value-laden and subjective. It will conjure up a variety of different interpretations and associated emotions for different people. One way of clarifying your initial reaction to this concept is to think about the opposite end of the nurturing/not nurturing spectrum. When someone is not being nurturing in their daily relationship with a child, what are they being? Think of a word or phrase that best describes your opposite of nurturing.

Ben is playing with his favourite toy animals at a Saturday play and craft group. He is busy lining up a row of sheep and then loading them one by one into a plastic truck. When Jack sits down next to him Ben pushes him away forcefully, saying 'You can't play!' Jack picks up the truck and carries it away. Ben begins to cry. Morag watches from a distance for a few moments and then silently offers Ben the doll that she has been playing with. When this doesn't help in abating his tears she briefly puts her arm around him and then goes to fetch Ben's mother, who has left the room to have a cup of tea. Mel rushes back to console Ben, expressing her guilt at having left him. Morag continues to watch Ben, evidently very distressed by his tears (see also Plummer, 2008, p.22).

With the background knowledge that we already have about these children, we can begin to see different motivations for the nurturing strategies employed by both Morag and Mel. For example, our previous encounters with Morag might suggest to us that Morag's mother suffers from bouts of depression. She may, at times, be unresponsive to Morag's emotional needs. Morag is ambivalent and insecure in her relationship with her mother and, in consequence, has become very sensitive to other people's mood changes. Perhaps Mel is stressed about Ben's developmental delay. In fact, she is beset by feelings of guilt.

In discussion with the play leader, Mel offers 'not being there' (emotionally or physically) as her opposite of 'nurturing'. By exploring each of these two poles in more depth she finds that, for her, 'being there' all the time has the potential to tip into over-protection. She recognises that this could prevent Ben from learning to problem-solve and to take appropriate risks, perhaps leading to him becoming inappropriately fearful of many 'normal' activities. With some support she is able to make the first steps towards re-visioning her image of 'nurturing' to include a greater element of safe exploration and experimentation for Ben.

Nurturing can embody slightly different *qualities* according to circumstances and according to the age and stage of individual children.

Neuro nugget

Research neuroscientist Lise Eliot cites a study undertaken by researchers at the University of Washington who compared frontal-lobe EEG measures (EEG (electroencephalography) involves the recording of electrical brain activity via electrodes placed on the scalp) in the infants of depressed and non-depressed mothers. They found that by about one year of age, babies whose mothers were depressed showed a different pattern of neural responsiveness than control babies. During playful interactions, they experienced less activation of the left hemisphere (the 'feel-good' side) than control babies (Eliot, 1999).

Elaborating the construct of nurturing

Feeling nurtured as a child (not just the actual experience of being nurtured) will also have shaped your ideas about being a nurturing adult. You may perhaps have a drive to move *towards*, or to expand upon, the values and ideals that were the best of what you experienced as a child. Or it could be that your motivation is influenced by the wish to move *away* from some of the attitudes and behaviours of adults in your childhood – to be different, to do it all better. For many of us, our experiences lead us to being motivated by a combination of both these aspects.

Whether you are primarily motivated by moving towards something that you do want, or by moving away from something that you don't want, it is helpful to formulate a picture of your goals and to elaborate on this as much as possible.

The elaboration of what we want in life is not as straightforward as you might think. For example, we are often all too familiar with the intricate details of feeling stressed or put under pressure. When we experience too much pressure in our lives we can perhaps describe the emotions, physical sensations and behaviours that we manifest in some detail. But what about the sensations, feelings and behaviours associated with *not* being unduly stressed? It is not always so easy to elaborate the other side of the paradigm, in this instance the wellness aspect of our lives. (I am using wellness as a very broad term, since each of us will have different ideas about what wellness means too! Someone who is experiencing the stress of a long-term illness for instance is likely to have different parameters for wellness to someone who is physically healthy but currently feeling overly stressed). Focusing on elaboration of what we *don't* want has the unfortunate consequence of keeping it uppermost in our minds; it doesn't allow us the space to create movement and change in the desired direction. In a way, it is rather like me saying to myself at the start of a presentation: 'Don't think about your itchy nose' or saying to a child: 'Don't drop that cup.' An alternative picture would be more useful: 'Focus on the audience' or: 'Carry the cup carefully.'

If I want to be a nurturing adult, supporting well-being in the children with whom I work, or for whom I have a caring role, then I need to ask myself what that actually involves *for me*. As with the example of stress, if we simply try to think about what makes a person an effective supporter we might be tempted to drift into negatives: 'I don't want to be like X; they never took the trouble to listen to my worries.' If this happens we can ask ourselves what the opposite would be. Perhaps something like: 'Nurturing involves taking children's worries and concerns seriously.'

When I have a clear picture of what it is to be supportive and nurturing, it is easier for me to hold this in mind and to notice the times when I succeed and the times when it has been harder to fulfil my aspiration. When we make mistakes, this gives us the chance to review the situation calmly and set ourselves back on track. Everyone has the capacity to nurture, including those who have missed out on important nurturing relationships.

EXPLORATORY ACTIVITY 9.2:
QUALITIES AND INTERACTIONS

Take some time to consider what it is that you hope to gain from your nurturing interactions with children. Do you want to inspire them? Help them to negotiate the world more successfully? Entertain them? Build strong bonds? Enjoy their company? Teach/support them effectively? Take a moment to jot down a few ideas.

Now think of people in your life whom you felt offered these things to you. For example, was there anyone in your childhood who inspired you to do something? This could be someone you knew personally or perhaps someone famous – an inspirational athlete or a television presenter for example. Was there a teacher or a member of your family who taught you something that has stayed with you all your life? Write down the names of these important people.

Think about the qualities that these people possessed. These might be qualities that you recognised as a child or qualities that you have only realised later on in life. For example, you might have been inspired by someone who was a good listener and really took time to hear about your wishes and dreams – someone who encouraged you, helped you to find out more about what you wanted to do. Perhaps you knew someone who had a great sense of fun or adventure or someone who had endless patience. If you were inspired by someone in the public eye, what was it about their personality that inspired you? Was it perseverance, courage, joyfulness? Try to think about these qualities without adding any ifs and buts. Think of them as a child would, without concerns such as 'He/she couldn't possibly have been like that all the time!'

Think about the type of interactions that you had and the activities that you did together. For example, did you read together? Tell stories? Build dens? Carry out experiments? Bake cakes? Go for walks? Play quiet games? Play noisy games? Did they take the lead? Did you choose the activities? Were you usually with other children? Did you have special time with a grandparent/parent on your own? Again, if you have someone famous in mind then think about why they particularly captured your attention. Did they inspire you with what they said, the way that they put their ideas across or perhaps by their actions in the community?

Pause now to reflect on what you have written with regard to personal qualities and types of interaction.

STORY-BUILDING ACTIVITY 9.1: A CHARACTER PROFILE

Based on your exploration of nurturing qualities, sketch out a 'character profile' for a nurturing figure in a puppet play or an oral story. What qualities will you want to emphasise?

In summary, when we construct a story about nurturing, we need to consider the following points:

- What is the child's/group's background?
- What does *this* child/group of children need from the story?
- How will I tell or show the positive aspects of nurturing?
- How will I tell or show that everyone can make mistakes in nurturing others and in nurturing ourselves and that it is important to learn from these mistakes?

References

Eliot, L. (1999) *What's Going on in There? How the Brain and Mind Develop in the First Five Years of Life*. New York: Bantam.

Gerhardt, S. (2004) *Why Love Matters: How Affection Shapes a Baby's Brain*. London and New York: Routledge.

Plummer, D. (2008) *Social Skills Games for Children*. London and Philadelphia: Jessica Kingsley Publishers.

CHAPTER 10

Stories about Skills and Qualities and Facing Challenges

Aisha: I like being at home using Daddy's computer. I am really good at all the games and I know about all sorts of things that even Daddy doesn't know. I write stories on the computer too. Sometimes when it's bedtime I am in the middle of something important and I get cross that I have to stop.

We build our confidence in our own abilities over a lengthy period of time and by trial and error. The process is dependent on the development of certain cognitive abilities such as the abilities to compare oneself with others, to make distinctions between actual and ideal self-concepts, to view things from different perspectives and to understand the difference between effort and ability (Harter, 1999). We are also heavily influenced in this process by our daily experiences and by the verbal and non-verbal feedback from important people in our personal environments.

For some children, this idea of gradual progress can be very difficult to grasp. Youngsters may have older siblings who are racing ahead with their skills. Children may not recognise their strengths in a particular area if all their focus is on something that their peers can already do successfully.

EXPLORATORY ACTIVITY 10.1: APPRECIATING YOUR SKILLS AND QUALITIES

In the centre of a large piece of paper write the name of the child or children who you are focusing on at the moment as a parent, carer or practitioner. Around the outside of the paper write all the roles that you currently perform in relation to this child or children. As an alternative, you could draw a representation of these roles, rather than write them out.

Choose one role. Think about the qualities and skills that you have that help you to fulfil this role. Be specific and try not to qualify your thoughts with 'ifs' or 'buts' ('I am patient...but sometimes I get so tired that his constant requests for bedtime stories drive me nuts!').

I wonder how comprehensive your list is. Most people will struggle a little with this unless they have done a similar exercise before. It is often hard for us to acknowledge our skills and there may be skills and qualities that you have forgotten to add. So now I invite you to think about a leisure activity or hobby that you really enjoy. This doesn't need to be something that you are necessarily very good at – perhaps it is something you are still learning. The key point is that it is something that you enjoy. What qualities and skills do you have that enable you to enjoy this pastime? Write your ideas on a second piece of paper.

Do this again for at least two more activities that you enjoy.

Have you thought of anything that was not on your skills and qualities list for the roles you fulfil with children? If so, are there any that you can now add to your first piece of paper?

STORY-BUILDING ACTIVITY 10.1: PYRAMIDS AND TASKS

Think of a child who is keen to develop a particular skill or attribute. Imagine yourself in this child's shoes. What might they consider constitutes this skill? (Of course, if you want to, you could do this exercise with the child and get her own perspective first hand.) Draw out a pyramid (see Exploratory activity 4.3: Creativity pyramid) and then choose three skills or attributes from this pyramid that seem achievable. Make a note of these as being potential elements of three tasks for a story.

Exploratory activity 10.1 illustrates the inter-relatedness of our skills. It reflects one of the principles of solution focused brief therapy (e.g. Berg and de Shazer, 1993) – the belief that a person who is seeking to make changes in her life will already be doing something, however small, towards making that desired change, although she may not necessarily be consciously aware of this. The activity also highlights a basic principle of working with others – it makes sense to start from a person's strengths in order to help her to find the best ways in which to tackle more challenging aspects of her life. This is one of the many lessons that I learnt from parents of children in therapy – they often came to therapy with a sense of feeling disempowered, concerned at the amount of jargon and 'specialist' knowledge that they thought they might need in order to support their children. This is a misconception that all therapists are quick to try and dispel but I am aware that this feeling can still linger in some families and add to the already stressful situations that many are facing. Starting from a family's strengths rather than what might be problematic is the most common-sense way forward.

GENERAL ADAPTATIONS

- The activity can be done with parents/carers in a group or individually. Discussions could then centre on the range and depth of ideas engendered and how these personal skills and qualities might be utilised in everyday life and in difficult situations.

- The activity can be adapted to help adults reflect on the skills and qualities of individual children. I like to use an 'asset jigsaw' for the children's version. This is just a blank template of a jigsaw with six to eight pieces. In order to complete the jigsaw, each person thinks of at least three things that his/her child enjoys doing. They then think about what 'skill' or quality (asset) their child has that enables them to enjoy this pastime. Each 'asset' is entered in the jigsaw. The group discusses how many of these could be used when tackling a problem in a different area of life. Questions for discussion could be based around 'What would you most like other people to know about your child? What do you appreciate about him/her? What are his/her skills and qualities?' Looking at how one skill can support different endeavours can help to ease the pressure of trying something new. In the following interchange, Laura helps Aisha to see the value of watching/observing as another way of learning and makes it clear that she has some choice about when to join in.

Laura: You've done really well to go to dance classes with the other children.

Aisha: I don't like it.

Laura: I know. You don't like the class. I guess that's because you're not sure about the dancing. Everyone else has been there longer than you have.

(Aisha nods.)

Laura: Do you remember on your jigsaw picture you put 'good at looking' as one of your strengths? You are so good at watching and learning. I think the dancing will get easier for you. Shall we do some practice at home too?

- The asset jigsaw can be used with individual children to help them to explore their own strengths or with groups, where the aim is to highlight the important contribution of individual assets to a team, class or therapy group. They may want to draw a representation of skills rather than write about them. Hearing yourself talk about something that you like about yourself can be a very positive experience. The flipside of this is that recognising and talking about your positive qualities is often difficult, particularly for vulnerable children and particularly if they confuse appreciation with 'boasting', which may result in negative reactions from their peers. The asset jigsaw can be quite small to start with but can be left open sided so as to allow for additions as and when appropriate. Each new or expanded skill or strength should be related back to a variety of different situations and tasks. A child is much more likely to develop her skills further or to be motivated to learn new skills if she can see the personal benefits of doing so.

- A skills 'cloak' can also be used – this could be real, with pictures pinned to it, or imaginary. Perhaps a child will imagine herself putting on her skills cloak when she is about to undertake a new task.

Remember, children often fail to recognise their skills and how these can contribute to their learning. Just as you might teach skills such as doing up a coat or tying shoelaces by first demonstrating and then encouraging a child to do it with help and eventually on her own, so too might you show through stories how protagonists learn skills in stages in order to overcome an obstacle. Stories about how a protagonist's unique but previously unrecognised skill helps a community to achieve something together are also useful.

Other story ideas

- Stories highlighting the difference between recognising and appreciating skills in yourself and others in contrast to boasting.

- Stories illustrating how skills are transferable.

- Stories about appreciating a skill or quality for its own sake, without the need to 'achieve' any particular goal, other than enrichment of life.

References

Berg, I. K. and de Shazer, S. (1993) 'Making Numbers Talk: Language in Therapy.' In S. Friedman (ed.) *The New Language of Change: Constructive Collaboration in Psychotherapy.* New York: Guilford Press.

Harter, S. (1999) *The Construction of the Self.* New York: Guilford Press.

CHAPTER 11

Stories about Building Knowledge and Confidence

It is usually the case that our learning is influenced by a variety of ideas from different sources. As we come into contact with each new child and his family, and with each new theory and strategy, we may confirm or deepen our own approaches, or occasionally even find ourselves questioning our core principles. We may realise, for example, that some of our ideas might be 'received wisdom' – 'I can't remember where I got that from', 'Everyone knows that's a helpful way to respond to a distressed child' and so on.

Other influences on the ways in which we support children may come from intuitive knowledge that is based on our previous experiences. Making this tacit knowledge *explicit* helps us to evaluate what we do in a creative and mindful way.

My framework for working with children is grounded in my training as a speech and language therapist and over the years my ideas and strategies have been greatly influenced through engagement with teachers and mentors from many other disciplines. It has been an exciting journey, my work constantly evolving in response to the ways in which children, colleagues and students engaged with the ideas or, conversely, found it difficult to connect with them. I recognise that it has also been a very personal journey. Below, I have suggested a few activities to help you to identify your personal framework. Your beliefs, learning and experiences are paramount in informing your use and adaptations of the ideas that have been presented throughout this book. Even if you feel that you are already clear about your viewpoints, I encourage you to explore this further. Having quiet times for reflection and consolidation in this way is important for us as supporters and is vital to bear it in mind for children too. Children need time to pause and reflect, to understand the relevance of their achievements and learning, before moving on to the next targets. They need time to build their 'expert' knowledge and to feel comfortable with an activity *not because they are children*, but because all of us, at any age, benefit from the opportunity to practise the skills that we are developing so that we can then structure our own learning.

EXPLORATORY ACTIVITY 11.1: THE LEARNING TREE

Think about any discussions or training that you have undertaken or any books that you have read that you feel have influenced your approach to supporting children.

Imagine that this experience and knowledge can be depicted as a tree – the trunk represents the main element of your knowledge and beliefs and the branches represent the additional ideas or people that have influenced you. Add as many branches as you like. Try to include some that you may not have thought of as relevant before. Remember that the shape of trees can change and new branches can be added. Trees also have lumps and bumps that add to their character. Whatever insights you may gain from doing this activity, view them as extra information that will help you with your interactions.

In discussing learning trees with other people it has been clear that a major theme in personal learning and its application to supporting children is the imperative to *make one's own life as rich and varied as possible*. We can draw from many sources in our endeavours to build supportive relationships with children and should not underestimate the contribution of our own joys in engaging with sports, literature, art or any other creative pursuits.

While writing this book I also revisited my own learning tree. I thought about the people who influenced my work, about ideas that I tried to integrate into my therapy and teaching, and those which I struggled to incorporate because they did not fit with my view of therapeutic support. I wondered why it had taken me so long to hear about some ideas that, when I did finally stumble upon them, seemed so inspirational, innovative or just to be sound common sense! I once again realised the importance of learning from *doing*. No amount of academic learning can substitute for practical experience.

GENERAL ADAPTATIONS

- This is a simple activity to do with children. You could use the concept of a tree to help children to identify the main people and events that have influenced who they are and how they see the world. While this would be particularly useful for older children who might be quite elaborate or abstract in their construction, it can be helpful for younger children to explore their world in this way too.

*Aisha identified her parents as the main trunk of her tree. She also included her grandmother as being important. She could not think of anyone else to add. I asked her about big events in her life and she told me that recently a van from the local radio station had come to school to talk to one of the teachers. She told me about the excitement in the school and said that the reporter had asked her (Aisha) a question but she didn't know what to say and so had missed the chance of being on the radio. This was evidently an important event for Aisha and was uppermost in her mind because of its recency. She expressed a mixture of feelings, but mostly anger towards the reporter. My sense was that she had felt frustrated with herself and had **experienced** this as anger. We added 'radio visit' as a branch quite high up on her tree.*

- You might use a drawing of a tree to help a child to identify and verbalise aspects of their environment that help them to learn. For example, Aisha might identify 'quietness' or 'being calm' as the main trunk of her tree with branches such as 'a quiet space to do homework' and 'time on my own'.

STORY-BUILDING ACTIVITY 11.1: STORY TREES

When you come to construct a story or set of stories with a child a story tree will help him to identify themes and intentions. In order to see how this might work you could construct one for yourself first. As an example, the trunk of a story tree might be 'worries' or 'making friends'. The branches might represent different aspects that will appear in your story/stories around this theme. Or perhaps the trunk is a skill or quality that is important to a child and the branches are different story ideas based around this. Laura drew a story tree for Aisha.

The trunk was 'making friends' and 'finding courage'. The branches were gradually filled with skills and challenges that I wove into stories at different times. Later I used the same idea to encourage Aisha to draw her own story tree and put things in her own words. She drew a tree with the trunk labelled 'quietly brave'. Her own ideas for stories showed me how much she valued her quiet times and her need to be with like-minded friends. This prompted me to take Aisha and two of her friends to hear a story-teller in the park. They enjoyed it so much that we are going to start a small story-telling circle at home.

Mel's story tree for Ben centred on hospital visits. Ideas that she wanted to weave into the stories included meeting new people, feeling safe in a new place and being helped to get better. She made up very short stories incorporating one idea at a time and using Ben's favourite farm animals to 'act out' the story. Ben later started to retell these stories when playing on his own.

And, of course, trees can feature in stories too, where they often signify strength, rootedness or wisdom.

CHAPTER 12

Stories about Gaining Mastery and Achieving Goals

Neuro nugget

Researchers appear to have identified a particular gene that is involved in the utilisation of three important psychological resources for coping with stress and depression: mastery (the belief that one has control over one's own life), self-esteem and optimism. The gene in question is an oxytocin receptor (Saphire-Bernstein *et al.*, 2011). Oxytocin is a hormone known to aid the 'bonding' process after childbirth. It induces feelings of calmness and is also associated with empathy and positive social interactions. Levels of oxytocin vary enormously according to how much positive physical contact we experience.

EXPLORATORY ACTIVITY 12.1: LOCUS OF CONTROL

In exploring your 'life path' (Exploratory activity 5.3), how much did you feel in control of what is happening in your life and between you and your child or the children with whom you work? Note down anything that comes to mind when you think of the word 'control'.

We each have different views about the amount of control we are able to exercise in our own lives. This is influenced by our natural temperament, our culture and our lifetime experiences. Some people have a strong internal locus of control. They use language that reflects the belief that they are the masters of their own fate: 'My achievements are due to my hard work.' They also use 'I' statements, rather than 'You' statements. For example, a statement such as 'You make me so angry,' assumes a very different locus of control to 'I feel angry about what you just said/did.' Some people are more inclined to look externally for the reasons behind events in their life such as powerful others (health professionals, government and so on) or fate: 'It's just luck of the draw.'

Most children have very limited experiences of being in control of their own life. They are generally told what to do, think and say and when to do it. They find it difficult to make decisions or to take responsibility for their actions: 'David made me do it!' This is a natural part of growing up. Becoming healthily independent and able to make informed choices is a slow and steady process. It requires a fine balance between leading and supporting. If adult guidance is relinquished too soon, the experience of having a high degree of control in their lives at an early age can be overwhelming for some children.

GENERAL ADAPTATION OF EXPLORATORY ACTIVITY 5.3: LIFE PATHS

Formulating and working towards personal goals is an important factor in building mastery in one's own life. Life paths can also be used as an aid to identifying strategies for achieving both short- and long-term goals. In this version the 'explorer' walks *back* along a *future* stretch of the path to points that are a few hours, days or weeks apart, ending at the present moment (literally, imagining a line along the floor that starts at a designated point in the future such as finishing college, taking an exam or dealing with a tricky situation at school). In essence, she is retracing her steps *as if* the event had already taken place. The time intervals should be small enough to be manageable but large enough to give the explorer the opportunity to carry out a small task or complete a small element of the overall goal. At each point, the facilitator asks questions and makes comments that will help the explorer to identify useful coping strategies.

Tom: Your teacher told me you've just given your talk on positive aspects of social media. How did it go?

Ardan: It was okay. I feel good about it. I was nervous but I was well prepared. (Ardan then moves back along the line to a pre-agreed point that, in this instance, represents two days earlier. Tom orientates Ardan by talking about which day of the week it is and whether it's morning or afternoon.)

Tom: I hear you're giving a presentation in two days. Tell me about what you are doing at the moment to help you to prepare.

Ardan: I haven't got much time to prepare today but last night I put the finishing touches to it so that I can run through the whole thing with my dad tonight and get the timing right.

(Ardan moves back along the line a little further)

Tom: You've got less than a week to get a presentation together. How's it going?

Ardan: I've written the basic script and today I finished the graphics. I always get nervous about presentations so I'm making sure I'm prepared enough to be able to make any last minute changes without panicking.

And so on.

This activity can be done with children as young as four or five if you make the steps very manageable.

Neuro nugget

The ability of the nervous system to modify its organisation and function throughout an individual's lifetime is commonly referred to as plasticity. The plasticity of the brain and the way in which it can form new neuronal connections is well documented. It has been found that new connections can be formed simply by imagining doing something over and over again. In this way, the imagination can affect actual ability, such as learning to play the piano or to play golf.

Imagine that Morag wants to go to swimming lessons with her friends but is fearful of taking the first step. The life-path and goal-setting activities can both be used as a basis for a story or puppet play to help her to move towards achieving her goal. Jo chose to use a conversation between two puppets to portray the small steps and the emotions involved in making a start on something that is scary for one of them.

Children will also need to know (explicitly and from experience) that you will encourage them to move on to something new or slightly more challenging *when you feel that they are ready*. This is not only relevant for school targets, but also for general life experiences. We can encourage children to think about the ways in which even small steps in their learning contribute in a wider sense to shaping the ways in which they think and behave.

> *Jo: Morag, what did you like about the game we have just played?*
>
> *Morag: It was fun.*
>
> *Jo: You had fun learning about how to listen.*
>
> *(Morag nods.)*
>
> *Jo: Isn't it lovely to feel that! You are good at joining in with games (pause) and you are listening really well. Having fun while you are learning new things helps you to remember them (pause). Our brains remember things more easily when we are having fun.*

You might already have a situation in mind that could be addressed using this approach. If not, imagine that you are Laura for a moment. Aisha has been asked to write a short biography of a famous person for homework. She is having difficulties choosing from the many options of famous people and is feeling overwhelmed and anxious about managing to complete the task on time. Using the example of the goal-setting activity demonstrated by Tom and Ardan, in which the explorer starts from the end point and travels back to a starting point, have a go at making up a short story about a famous (unspecified) character taking a child back in time to help her to complete her task (or you may want to base the story around two animals or two puppets). Having a brief outline at this stage will help you with later activities but, once again, there is no right or wrong way of doing this.

Imagining an event *as if* it has already happened successfully gives a powerful message to the unconscious – something that most athletes can attest to. And as we also know, imagining ourselves failing or doing badly in some future event can affect our actual performance too, so it makes sense to train ourselves to form more useful, proactive images.

Some ideas for stories related to this theme

- Working towards goals with a helper.
- 'Standing up' for something you believe in strongly.
- Coping with unexpected events.

References

Saphire-Bernstein, S., Way, B. M., Kim, H. S., Sherman, D. K. and Taylor, S. E. (2011) 'Oxytocin receptor gene (OXTR) is related to psychological resources.' *PNAS (Proceedings of the National Academy of Sciences of the United States of America) 108*, 37.

CHAPTER 13

The Next Steps

Adapting and extending stories and puppetry

One of the many skills inherent in a creative approach to engaging with children lies in developing the confidence to adapt or 'play with' activities and strategies in order to make them maximally effective for individuals.

EXPLORATORY ACTIVITY 13.1: ADAPTING ACTIVITIES

Think of an activity that you like to use with children. Run through this activity in your mind. Imagine yourself and a child or group of children engaging with it. Enjoy the feelings that are engendered by an activity that is effective and pleasurable. Imagine that the activity is over and you are reflecting on how you might now adapt it to suit different needs, incorporating stories or puppetry. What are your first thoughts?

There are many ways in which to modify activities in order to make them more inclusive, to increase or decrease their complexity or to change their main focus so as to extend their range of usefulness. The following questions can be used as a starting point to help you to alter/adapt a story or puppet interaction to suit different needs and strengths.

Ask yourself the following questions:

- How can I increase/decrease the complexity of *one* element of the activity? Can I add to or subtract from the number of characters or the number of scenes? Can

I simplify the storyline? Can I remove distractions such as music, props or a complicated piece of scenery? Can I deliberately *add* a distracting element in order to help a child to extend his skills in focusing and attending?

- Can this activity be undertaken in a different environment? For example, if I normally tell stories indoors can I tell this one outside? Or in a story tent constructed in the classroom/living room?

- Could this activity be led by children, rather than me? Could it be led by a puppet? Could children teach each other a story? Could they teach me? Could they make up their own puppet play based on a learning target?

- How could I modify this activity to give it a different focus? For example, if it is primarily a story about looking closely at something or being mindful of the environment, how could I change it so that the focus is on listening instead?

- What might happen if I change the length of this activity? Could I extend it or shorten it?

- Could I vary the materials used in this activity and still fulfil my original aims? This variation could range from changing the category of the materials (glove puppets to shadow puppets) or changing the type within a category (crayons to paints). You can even incorporate technology by making MP3 recordings or computer-animated presentations of a story for a child to keep. I have done both these with children and heard later that they had sometimes been presented in 'show-and-tell' sessions.

Whenever I start to think about variations and adaptations for an activity, I can easily stray from the original aim or intended outcome. I see this as a useful process but when time is limited I write my aim on the top of a piece of paper and keep reminding myself of this as I jot down my thoughts. Sometimes, when I have thought about a particular aim for a while, I discard everything that I came up with, but a more useful idea will occur to me while I am doing something more relaxing such as walking the dogs. This is a common phenomenon: new ideas can occur to us when we are relaxing after a period of intense thought because we give our minds 'space' to be creative, *based on the work we have already done*. This is an important concept for children to understand as well. They may not always come up with the perfect solution to dealing with a problem while they are doing an activity with you, but they might reach a better understanding, and therefore a better way of dealing with that problem, at a later time. This is also why children can benefit from having wind-down periods to allow them the space for moments of insight. Quiet moments of relaxation after a period of intense concentration – time just to doodle, listen to quiet music or perhaps spend a few moments sitting in relaxed silence – can all be beneficial. The more experiences they have of engaging with creative problem-solving in this way, the more likely it is that they will experience moments of insight.

STORY-BUILDING ACTIVITY 13.1: REMEMBERING A STORY

There are some quick and easy ways to help you to remember the main sequence of events in a story or puppet show.

- Once you have your story or your script outline refine it down to fewer and fewer key words. A page of story might become six sentences and those six sentences can become six words. This will be much easier to remember!

- Use a small story box containing key elements of your story. These could be small figures, drawings or symbols to represent the different stages of the story. Before you start your story carefully unwrap the objects and lay them out in front of you – make it a special part of the story-telling process.

- Draw a large story 'map' plotting the journey that your protagonist will make. Lay this on the floor and 'walk' the journey e.g. from the castle to the mountains, to the wizard's cave and back to the castle.

STORY-BUILDING ACTIVITY 13.2:
REGULAR STORY TIMES

The following outline is useful for times that you have specifically scheduled for story-telling or puppetry with a group. This is easily adapted for use with individual children too. The main point is that the session is 'packaged' so that the format has structure and allows time for all the elements of a supportive environment to be put into place. Although I ask children to become 'still' before we begin, I do not expect them to remain still for the duration of the session. This request is just setting up a 'pause' in thought and action.

- Ask the children to sit quietly in the space designated for story-telling. Ask them to be as still as possible. Give them specific instructions about how to achieve this. For example, show them how to be aware of and to feel the flow of their breath in and out. Offer positive feedback on how well the group is achieving this, noting the benefits to the group as a whole. Avoid picking out individual children for this feedback; make it more generic, such as: 'I am noticing how calm the group can be when you are doing relaxed breathing.' Don't worry if there are some who find this aspect difficult. Some children will naturally become still and attentive within the space while others may take many weeks to get to this stage.

- Set the scene for the story or play with an introduction such as: 'Today we are going to hear a story about a little boy who liked to play in the mud.'

- Tell the story.

- Sit quietly for a few moments after the story so that the children can absorb what they have heard. You may find it useful to also incorporate a specific wind-down activity. For example, after a brief silence, you could finish with each person having the chance to say one sentence beginning with 'I felt…', 'I noticed that…' or 'The story was…'

- If you have scheduled enough time for reflection you could invite the children to draw a picture or an abstract representation. Younger children might simply draw something that happened in the story; older or more able children can be encouraged to draw something that somehow shows what they 'felt' or 'experienced' during the story. Invite the children to talk about their pictures if they would like to.

- Thank the children for their participation and offer brief, positive feedback.

- Finish with an affirming comment to the whole group about your own experience of sharing the story with them. For instance, 'Thank you. I really enjoyed our story-time together.'

- Make a link with the next or previous activity. There is no need to labour this point. Children will soon get used to the format and will be able to suggest their own links before long.

- 'Tiptoe' out of the space, or move quietly to the next activity.

A Story within a Story

We are about to go full circle with this book! Ben, Ardan, Aisha, Morag and the adults who supported them have taken part in a story about how we all struggle to make sense of our worlds, about the journeys we might undertake in pursuit of 'a better way of doing things', the mistakes we make along the way and the obstacles we overcome.

I started by saying that many people believe that supportive interactions with children constitute both science and art. While the principles in this book are based on learning and experience, the ways in which you engage with them and use them in your work, in your community or at home will involve your own insights and intuition. I hope that the four children have helped you with this. Once I had set them on their journeys in Chapter 2, their stories seemed to unfold of their own accord. Each child clamoured for more attention than the others at certain points in the book; each of them challenged me in different ways while I was writing about them. In my head they each have a very full life story and very unique personalities. It is surprisingly difficult to stop thinking about what might come next for them! However, I thank them and entrust them into your care so that they can continue to grow and flourish in your own imaginations and help you to develop your own versions of the 'in-between'.

And now, I tiptoe quietly out of the space…